It's Your Own Time You're Wasting

Freddy Quinne

TABLE OF CONTENTS

PREFACE	iii
CHAPTER 1	1
CHAPTER 2	14
CHAPTER 3	33
CHAPTER 4	49
CHAPTER 5	67
CHAPTER 6	74
CHAPTER 7	89
CHAPTER 9	123
CHAPTER 10	135
CHAPTER 11	147
CHAPTER 12	160
CHAPTER 13	175
CHAPTER 14	184
CHAPTER 15	192
CHAPTER 16	205
CHAPTER 17	218
CHAPTER 18.	229
CHAPTER 19	239
CHAPTER 20	248
CHAPTER 21	257
EPILOGUE	278

PREFACE

I think that the reader wants to come away from the book thinking that teachers are heroes; not that the profession is full of cliques and backstabbing shits. This is one of the first pieces of feedback I ever got about this book. And, after hundreds of comments, corrections, rewrites and restructures, it's the one that has stuck with me the most.

For a start, the profession *is* full of cliques and backstabbing shits. There's no getting around that; and any teacher who tells you otherwise is either straight up lying or has been fortunate enough to only work in departments where everyone gets along, and the chance of the latter is roughly the same as winning the lottery, being struck by lightning and then being eaten by a shark all in the same day. So very, very unlikely - unless you're at a newsagents in the middle of a thunderstorm whilst on a day trip to the Sealife Centre holding hands with the tin man from Wizard of Oz.

Teaching is full of incredible, kind, courteous, courageous, inspiring folk, but it also has its fair share of dickheads. Most jobs are like that. My partner is a Deputy Ward Manager at a mental health clinic, which means she's usually the one in charge of all the patients and staff. Now, it goes without saying that to work in mental health you need to be an exceptional human being with an array of skills. I certainly couldn't deal with being screamed at all hours of the day by someone throwing their own shit at you. It's one of the reasons I don't have kids.

And yet, despite these people needing superhuman empathy, patience and understanding just to get through their shifts, the staff can be surprisingly vicious to one another. Like a fat man in a Lycra catsuit, there's often a lot of tension and things can snap at any moment. I asked my partner why she thought her employees acted this way and her answer was one of philosophical elegance - "they spend so much time giving all their compassion to the patients, they don't have any left for one another."

Teaching is very much the same - it's a high pressure, high performance job and this can manifest negative behaviours. Obviously we can't direct that negativity at the kids, and so quite often we deflect it onto one another. I don't want you to think that every teacher is an arsehole, that's not the case whatsoever, but neither is it a profession full of saints. Some teachers are always wonderful, some are always awful, and most of us are somewhere in-between. We have good days and bad days, just like everyone else. The only profession where you're surrounded by saints is as a footballer at Southampton.*

I also question why people might have this need to see teachers as heroes. They certainly aren't treated like heroes - neither are doctors, nurses, carers, firemen, police or any of the other supposedly noble professions - and they damn sure aren't paid like heroes. In fact, the only time any of these people are treated like heroes is by holding them up to a higher moral standard than everyone else in society.

Teachers in particular are not supposed to have a life outside of the classroom. I've known teachers who are given written warnings for having bikini pictures on their personal instagram pages. One female member of staff even lost her job after a single photo of her doing a topless modelling shoot from over a decade ago was found by a pupil. In all instances action was brought after pressure from parents. Perhaps instead of punishing adults for having past lives, we should be using this time to teach children about body objectification and sexual agency.

I too have faced major issues because of my comedy background (but you'll have to read on to find out more.. I wouldn't want to spoil it for you) and one of the aims of this book is to ask the reader at what point teachers should be granted the right to fulfil external hobbies and interests without it damaging the perception of their professional capabilities. Should an Assistant Headteacher be allowed to indulge in nudism on weekends? Could a Physics teacher be allowed to realise a dream of becoming a grime artist?

Moonlighting under the pseudonym MC Squared?

And why is it teachers that are subjected to this higher bar of extracurricular integrity in the first place? Why don't we demand the same of bankers? The financial sector held the respect of the community for hundreds of years, and yet we allow them to do copious amounts of cocaine and visit strip clubs every weekend since the 80s without calls to resign over their behaviour. Hell, they pretty much sent the global economy into a recession in 2008 and nobody batted an eyelid. You might say "well teachers look after children", and that's true, but bankers look after money. And whilst most value our kids more than our savings, it's not true of everyone. That's why not every kidnapping gets paid a ransom.

Perhaps the reason teachers and bankers aren't held to the same moral standard is because we want to fetishise the former as heroes in a way we don't with the latter. And therein lies my second point - if we want to encourage more people to get into teaching we should probably be making it more accessible by allowing teachers the luxury to pursue other interests and not be vilified for doing so.

Finally, and perhaps most pertinently of all, maybe it's time for us to redefine the word 'hero'. Currently we think of knights in shining armour, or people with superpowers and great teeth saving cities from peril. You never see Superman having a bad day, wandering aimlessly round the city because he can't find the address of the crime he's supposed to stop. Spiderman's alarm never goes off late so he doesn't have time for a shower and instead has to make do with roll-on deodorant, meaning he spends all day paranoid about whether or not people can smell him. Heroes are supposed to be infallible. Incapable of mistake or error. Perfect.

Trying to compare a mere human to these standards means they will inevitably fall short. By putting them on a pedestal you are setting them up to fail. In the words of Batman ally-cum-nemesis Harvey Dent - "you either die a hero, or you live long enough to see yourself become a villain." Thankfully the number of teachers killed in active duty each year is infinitesimally small, removing a Year 10s gym bag from a classroom is about as close as we'll get to diffusing a dirty bomb, but the flip side of that is that most of us stay in the profession long enough to see ourselves painted as the enemy at some point or another.

This is almost always done by the right wing politicians and media, who apparently view seeing a teacher doing something untoward as being as scandalous as catching the pope having a wank. It's a bitter pill for many to swallow, and almost certainly contributes to a culture of mistrust and ill-feeling to those in the job from people of certain socio-economic backgrounds. I can't imagine anyone quits solely off the back of this treatment, but it certainly doesn't help matters either.

The answer therefore, is to reevaluate what the word 'hero' should really mean. Suppose we do away with the flashy superpowers and the faultless facade. Perhaps being a hero isn't about saving the world or stopping an apocalypse; rather it's about turning up to work every day, knowing you're going to be rushed off your feet, putting in extra hours to get the job done, realising you might not always get the 'thank you' that you deserve. There is nobility in sacrifice. Being a hero is about having the courage to get things wrong and learn from them. It's about knowing you might not always get to save the day, but even making a small difference to just one person can add up to something big later down the line. And it's about knowing you might not get to see those changes even though you planted the seeds for them to grow.

It is often said that the world needs more heroes. Maybe we just need to change the definition.

*That is the best joke in the book, by the way. Now I've gotten it out of the way early, it's all downhill from here I'm afraid.

CHAPTER 1

My first stand-up comedy gig was on March 3rd, 2007. It was a Monday night new act show at The Frog and Bucket in Manchester. For those of you unfamiliar with the live comedy scene, The Frog and Bucket's amateur show, known as Beat The Frog, is one of the most infamous comedy nights in the entire industry. Every household name, every TV comic, every circuit pro you saw at your work's Christmas-do that really made you howl but who's name you can't remember - they all did Beat The Frog.

What makes this particular night so special is the format of the show. Unlike a regular open mic night where vast swathes of would-be comedians go on stage and more often than not stink the room out for ten minutes apiece, Beat The Frog does it differently. They give out three big green cards to members of the audience. When the audience member doesn't like the act, they put their card up. The act's job is to try and last five minutes without all three cards going up. If you make the full five minutes you go into a clap-off at the end to decide a winner, but if the cards all go up together they cut your mic, play "Loser" by Beck (specifically the part that goes "I'm a loser baby, so why don't you kill me", because nothing thins out the herds of delusional wannabes quite like subliminal messaging) and you have to leave the stage. It's a wonderfully brutal pantomime where the copiously talented and completely mental square off against one another, and the audience are the ones who decide which bracket you fall into.

The comedians are all new, desperate for stage time and eager to impress. When you're a newbie (also called an open spot), the first couple of years is a real slog. It's endless drives to the middle of nowhere to perform in front of three people and a dog, and the dog being the only one that looked like it was enjoying your act. It's tireless networking with people who run gigs, negotiating for stage time, currying favour with anyone who can put you in front of a crowd. To win Beat The Frog, or even to just last the five minutes, is a kernel of validation. It's the purest form of hope; a slither of light in an ocean of late night motorway drives and stale service station pasties. Even though you don't win any money, or a little trophy, or even so much as a swimming badge you can sew into your underwear, it represents a hell of a lot. It means you're *not* crazy for doing this, you've got talent.

I first heard about this night from two of my friends who were at Manchester University. I wanted to go to Manchester too but I didn't get the grades so I had to settle for University of Central Lancashire, which is kind of like wanting a glass of champagne but not having the money so having to settle for an old beer bottle that a tramp's pissed in. It's not that I wasn't clever, I was in the top sets at school, rather a case of me being like most young kids who are gifted with advanced cognitive ability - I was incredibly lazy.

Being lazy in secondary school is a trait you can quite easily get away with, providing you're savvy enough. Of course, you'll have to deal with the parents evenings and the school reports - *he's a clever lad, very academically capable, but he really needs to apply himself, or he won't get the GCSEs he wants, he needs to knuckle down, this year's an important one* - but if you can nod your head convincingly enough and make a few empty promises about self-improvement they'll leave you alone for a few terms until the next teacher comes along. Repeat that for 5 years and you're home dry.

I came out of school with pretty much the exact GCSEs I was predicted to get - mostly A's, a couple of B's and an E in Food Technology. I put absolutely no effort whatsoever into Food Tech, in fact I'd go as far as to say I analysed and identified the bar for minimum amount of work and gleefully limboed under it. One day we were given an assignment to come up with a new desert for a restaurant. We were given two hours to wow our teacher with our culinary creativity, who in turn was strutting up and down the classroom-come-kitchen like a Poundshop Paul Hollywood. By the time she'd gotten to my table, I was already done. I put some homemade custard in a bowl and stuck a cherry on top. Total preparation time - 30 seconds.

"Is this supposed to be finished?" My food tech teacher asked.

"Yep" I said, a tone of smugness in my voice that she couldn't possibly tell me off for finishing my work early, which I'm sure must have pissed her off no end.

"What's it called?"

I paused for a moment. "Strawberry Surprise."

"What's in it?"

"Cherries."

"So why is it called Strawberry Surprise?"

"Well," my voice raised loud enough so that everyone could hear the punchline, "the surprise is that it's a cherry".

With this in mind, it's a genuine surprise I even managed an E. It only makes you wonder how bad you have to be to *fail* that course, maybe she thought I'd made the custard myself and gave me points for that at least. My laissez-faire attitude was standard across all subjects, but in Food Technology I actively resented being there. I think this was because I never wanted to do it in the first place. Originally I'd asked to do I.T, but for some reason the school decided I should do Food Tech instead. I can only assume that, being quite a fat kid, they thought they were doing me a favour. Perhaps they imagined I'd see the grimy, germ ridden Food Tech classroom as some sort of contemporary Willy Wonka factory, and I'd be so overcome by gluttony that my head would get stuck in a jar or I'd drown in a chocolate fountain like a shit Augustus Gloop and the teachers would never have to deal with me again.

I coasted through high school getting by on the bare minimum and made it straight to college, where my lecturers quickly identified me as one of those "clever but lazy" types they'd seen a million times before and spent two years telling me how absolutely imperative it was that I pulled my finger out of my arse and did some actual work. Having been told something similar throughout high school (albeit without the metaphor of anal fingering) only to do fuck all and still end up with the exact same grades I was told I could only get by revising, I took their warnings with a pinch of salt. If anything, I wedged my entire hand up my rectum by regularly skipping classes to go to the bookies across the road.

When my A-Levels came round I thought I could just waltz through them and straight into whichever university I wanted. I'd already ruled out Oxford and Cambridge, not because I wasn't smart enough, but because I'd decided that these titanic bastions of education weren't up to my exacting standards. Too elitist. Too posh. With this in mind I'm sure the Oxbridge admission department lights a solitary candle in their offices every September to grieve over what might have been had I deemed them worthy.

Durham? Maybe. Sheffield? Perhaps. But two of my best mates were going to Manchester, so I decided to follow suit. I needed an A and two B's to get in. No problem. Like I said, I was a fat child, I'd had two B's since Year 8.

When I opened my results, I got three C's. I was crestfallen. All around me people were opening their results and their faces exploding with happiness. Some were ringing their parents, tears of joy streaming down their adolescent faces. I daren't even go home. I sat in the pub, my mates buying celebratory rounds and patting each other on the back, and I just remembered feeling completely and utterly numb. So much so, the University of Lancaster called my mobile phone (word of my dogshit results had clearly travelled quickly up the M6) and left a voicemail offering me a place studying English and Philosophy. I never called them back. Not that Lancaster wasn't a great uni, I was just too ashamed to speak to anyone.

I brushed it off by pretending I didn't give a fuck. In fact, I rode this angle so hard that it became a cornerstone of my personality. I began accepting dares and bets, and my mates were always taking advantage by concocting increasingly depraved challenges for me. One time they dared me to eat the world's hottest chilli pepper. Another time I tried viagra and went to a strip club. I took a perverse pride in conquering anything they put in front of me and the confidence it gave me, strutting round the place with no taste buds and a permanent erection. So when the call came in from one of my friends telling me about a stand up comedy competition I should enter, the gauntlet had been laid down and I duly accepted.

About a dozen of my friends came to watch my first gig. We all caught the train down together from Preston to Manchester, each with a four-pack of lager, determined to make a night out of it. Let's be clear - they weren't here for moral support. They wanted to watch me die on my arse in front of some people, laugh at me for a bit, then we could all get drunk. People kept asking me if I was nervous, I hadn't even comprehended this as a possibility. I didn't see what there was to be nervous about. It's not like I was fighting a tiger or flying with Ryanair. There's no danger here, it's just talking.

Given my proclivity for winging it, I hadn't bothered to google The Frog and Bucket. If I'd have stretched to doing even one iota of research I'd have found that it's one of the biggest comedy clubs in the country. I was expecting some little room above a pub, 20 people max. But as I walked to the bottom of Oldham Street, I saw a veritable comedy coliseum. My friends and I went inside and were greeted by a wall of noise, at least 300 audience members, and I swear to God at that moment I think I felt my arse hole pucker up and fold itself inside of me like a tiny piece of origami.

I was overcome with nervous energy, shaking uncontrollably. My hands became clammy. I could just about hear the compere talking to a fashion student in the front row, and he was getting some huge laughs from a raucous crowd. I was so consumed with my own stage fright that I'd zoned out to the point where they had to call my name twice before I started walking to the stage.

"So, you're the fashion student?" I asked a young girl in the front row.

"Yep."

"What bra size do you reckon I am?"

I can't remember anything else I said, but I won the competition.

After the show a man in a cheap suit offered me a gig in Withington in two days' time. I didn't

have the money to get the train back to Preston only to come back again 48 hours later, so I slept on my friend's floor for the two nights. I didn't bring a change of clothes, or a toothbrush, or spare underwear. But for those two days, I honestly thought I'd cracked comedy. Smash it in front of a few hundred on Monday, entertain a couple of thousand in Withington on Wednesday, probably get on telly by the weekend.

I rocked up to the gig in Withington smelling like an out of date tuna sandwich that had been left in a gym bag. There were six people in the audience. I strutted on stage, as confident as a man who'd just eaten chilli and viagra, and roundly died on my arse. Nothing I did or said was even close to being funny. I was caught like a deer in the headlights. So desperate was I for a laugh that at one point, I shit you not, I took my top off and licked one of my own nipples. I have no idea why I thought that would work, but rest assured, it didn't.

I caught the next train back home trying to work out which stunk up the room more, my act or my armpits. I couldn't work out how I could be so good one night and so poor the next. During the show I started chatting to another open spot who gave me a few names and numbers of other promoters in the area. The next day I had called them all and had a few more spots booked across the North West.

Over the following few months I did roughly twenty gigs across the UK. Most of them were horrendous - but a handful went well and that kept me going. But nothing ever matched the exhilaration of that first gig, no matter how much I chased it the high was never the same. I guess it's like a drug, in that way. Except instead of crack dens I was visiting motorway service stations. I envy the convenience of heroin addicts, at least they don't have to drive two hundred miles to Middlesbrough on a Wednesday for their fix.

After that I stopped comedy for a while. It's not that I'd fallen out of love with it, far from it, but I was struggling to reconcile with the horrible feeling of wanting to be really good at something but knowing you're really bad at it. All the other acts at my level were much older than me and they were talking about their wives and their kids and their jobs, and I couldn't really relate to any of that. I decided the reason that I sucked was because I didn't have enough life experience. Putting comedy temporarily on the shelf while I grew as a person felt like the right thing to do.

Three years went by before I felt ready to return to the stage. My time had been filled wisely - I'd dropped out of University to work full time at a job I fucking hated, has a couple of relationships with people I now fucking hated, and fallen madly in love only to have my heart broken. Feeling like I was ready to give things another shot, I booked a gig in for June 3rd 2010 and I've been a comedian ever since.

After about four years I was making enough money to think about going full time. In August 2014 I did the Big Value Comedy Showcase in Edinburgh, a well-known show for acts still establishing themselves which helps them get a taste of what Edinburgh has to offer. Then, off the back of that, I got myself an agent.

But by this point I'd realised that being a stand up comedian without any other skills or qualifications was a precarious existence. It's rather like those people you see walking a tightrope without a net or climbing a mountain without a rope - it looks like a thrilling and liberating lifestyle until you put a foot wrong and end up falling hundreds of feet with your body splashed across the floor like a Jackson Pollock painting.

As a newer act still forging your career, sometimes you'd work with older comics and it was hard to see them as anything other than a cautionary tale. Don't get my wrong, there's some fantastic club comics with distinguished careers that I really looked up to. But there were others who'd gone completely dead behind the eyes. They'd clearly fallen out of love with comedy years ago, but some of these people were in their 50s, with no transferable skills, and it was either get a job stacking shelves in a supermarket or drive to Hull for a hundred quid and keep pretending like the dream's still alive.

I remember working with one such act at a comedy club in Leeds. We were doing a weekend run together and it was someone I'd met before and gotten on well with. When I saw him in the dressing room on Friday night, he looked like a completely different person to the one I knew. I asked if everything was OK and he replied "Oh, it's my granddaughter's first birthday today. I had really wanted to be there, but then these shows came in, and I can't really turn work down at the moment." His face was stricken with pain, recalling the story whilst looking like he'd just stepped barefoot in lego. At that moment I stopped seeing him as a colleague, and instead a cautionary tale.

I didn't want to be one of those guys. I knew I needed another source of income that I could rely on - a steady job that I would enjoy that would allow me the freedom of working as a comedian at the weekends while providing me with a regular wage during the week, and a guaranteed pension when the time came to retire. I needed something that would put food on the table, something mortgage advisors wouldn't sneer at when hearing, and something that would make my Mum and Dad proud of me.

When I found out about teaching, I thought I'd discovered a job that ticked all of those boxes. What I didn't realise was that I'd stumbled across a world that everyone thinks they know but seldom truly understand, and it was about to turn my life upside down.

CHAPTER 2

From the looks of those slick "Get Into Teaching" adverts, you'd be forgiven for thinking the path into teaching was as easy as rocking up to any school in the country and signing a piece of paper promising not to molest anyone. In reality, the road to the classroom is a long and needlessly arduous one, fraught with obstacles along the way.

There are two main ways to gain your QTS (Qualified Teacher Status), the qualification that recognises you as a teacher. The first way is to apply through a university who'll teach you like it's a degree. There'll be a lot of PowerPoint, a lot of essays, a lot of time studying learning theories such as Vygotsy's Zone of Proximal Development. Then there'll also be some time spent in classrooms, trying desperately to cram facts about your subject of expertise to kids who could not give less of a shit.

The second way is to do what's called a Schools Direct course, which is basically a QTS degree run by a school (or collection of schools) with the intention of producing new teachers that they then get first dibs on. The Schools Direct scheme sees you spending significantly more time in the classroom with essays about learning theory spread thinly in-between like somewhat of an afterthought. The whole thing has a more vocational feel, you learn by doing.

The efficacy of the two systems is regularly debated. While they are in essence two sides of the same coin, they both spend an inordinate amount of time trashing the other's way of doing things. The university courses will tell you that you can't become a good teacher without a good grounding, and that months of theorising is necessary in order to properly contextualise the things you'll see in a classroom. The Schools Direct courses will tell you that you learn far more by getting your hands dirty, so to speak.

The way one Schools Direct course tutor summed it up to me was this - imagine you're drowning in the ocean and you get to choose one of two lifeguards to save you. The first lifeguard knew everything there was to know about swimming; they could identify undercurrents in the water, the proper technique to tread water for hours on end, even the exact angle that your arm should make contact with the water for maximum effectiveness, but they'd never actually stepped foot in a pool. The second lifeguard had been swimming for three hours a day every day for many years, but they couldn't so much as tell you the name of a swimming stroke. Who would you pick to come out and rescue you?

Whilst the approach from the universities and the Schools Direct courses differ greatly, one thing they both agree on is that they won't so much as entertain your application unless you've already spent a significant amount of time observing in a classroom. What this means is if you're to stand any chance of getting onto one of these courses you need to be in schools on a voluntary basis, and the more time you can get the better. This in itself is a stumbling block for many older people looking to get into teaching - it's simply not viable to take a month off work to go and sit in a classroom unpaid. You could, of course, take a year's worth of holiday leave in one go (if your employer is the reasonable sort that would allow that) but if you're someone with children that might not be an option either.

In theory, making sure people who want to become a teacher have spent time observing the job role isn't such a bad idea. It works for the universities and the Schools Direct schemes because they look and see you've made a commitment towards teaching, and it works for you because you get a taste of what you're letting yourself in for. But in reality, it's a largely pointless exercise.

If the purpose is to show your commitment to teaching, then we must recognise that this is wholly dependent on your personal circumstances. If you're married with kids, a job and a mortgage then yes, taking a month off to sit in a classroom and brush up on your GCSE French is very risky (or, if you prefer, tres risqué) and represents a serious decision on your part.

Conversely, if you're fresh out of university, live rent free with mum and dad and have no bills to pay, then it's hardly showing the same level of devotion.

But if the purpose is to get a fuller, more rounded view of the role of a teacher, then the classroom lessons you're observing are only one aspect of the job. What you won't see is all the admin and emails, the endless staff meetings, the tonnes of marking, lesson planning, and the million other things that are required of the modern day teacher. Observing a teacher when they're teaching and at no other point during the day is a bit like watching a footballer play for 90 minutes and assuming you've now got an overarching understanding of everything their job entails. There's a lot behind the scenes you don't see.

In order to arrange classroom observations the onus is on you to contact schools directly in order to negotiate this with them. While many schools try to be accommodating, there's really nothing in it for them. Your presence creates a slight amount of extra work as there's paperwork to fill out, passes to print off, emails to send and timetables to create for your visit, and there's not really anything you can offer in return. You just sit at the back of the class, smiling, trying to look as polite and respectable as you can.

Nobody sits down with you at any point and tells you *what* you should be observing. They don't tell you to watch how a teacher starts a lesson, or how they differentiate tasks based on ability, or how group work is structured, or how learning is evidenced, or behaviour is managed, or any of the fascinating mechanics behind being an effective teacher. You're not encouraged to interact with the pupils or to assist with their learning. You just sit there, not quite sure what you're doing, surrounded by a bunch of Year 8s who are also not quite sure what you're supposed to be doing, or if you're unlucky a bunch of Year 11s who'll take turns calling you a pedo behind your back just to see what you'll do.

Classroom observations get boring even more quickly than you might expect, so it's a good idea to come up with little internal games to keep yourself occupied. One thing I liked to do to pass the time was to see how quickly I could identify who the troublemakers were. Most of the time it's surprisingly easy, they'll come into class and within a few minutes will already be engaging in low level disruption - slamming bags onto desks, talking to their friends, generally being a nuisance. They don't try to hide it, quite the opposite, they relish the attention.

After a few days of shadowing one class in particular, I'd managed to get a pretty good read on the main characters. One pupil, Billy, stood out more than the others. It seemed like he was actively trying to be as naughty as possible without actually doing enough to get kicked out. It was a fine balancing act he pulled off with the grace and expertise of a seasoned circus performer walking an impossibly thin tight rope.

His favourite method of enacting his particular brand of havoc was to accuse his classmates of putting him off, playing the victim with such a commitment to method acting even Marlon Brando would be proud of. "Sirrrrr, James keeps breathing too loudly and I can't concentrate." He proclaimed one lesson, causing James to remonstrate that his respiratory system was operating at a perfectly normal volume. The class sat back and watched, now well versed in this particular pantomime.

"I've got sensitive ears!" Billy pleaded. "Sir, please make him move!"

"Why should I have to move? You move!" James shot back. Billy grinned, his plan working with a Machiavellian perfection you can't help but admire from a fourteen-year-old. The teacher, now faced with the dilemma on who to move between Billy and James, opted for a maverick third option, to get me to sit with them both. I don't know if you've ever had your own company used as a punishment before, but it's a pretty sobering moment.

I placed myself next to both lads and, to be fair to Billy, he had a point about James. Good Lord, the lad sounded like he was moving furniture. His body was a pile of involuntary wheezes and splutters, I felt like I was sitting next to the petrol engine of an old lawnmower. I watched Billy like a hawk, affixing him with as steely a glare as I could muster. He knew he was now under total surveillance, and it unnerved him. Reluctantly, he set about doing his work. Or at least, he tried to. He re-read his worksheet two or three times, tried putting pen to paper, but nothing came out. After a few minutes he gazed up at me, almost with a pleading look in his eye that said "help me."

We set about working on the problem together and once he'd figured out what he needed to do, he became a model student. He even helped old combustible steam engine James with his work too. I realised straight away the reason for Billy's misbehaviour - he was procrastinating. It's a trait I've often found in myself, if the work is too difficult I'll find reasons to put off doing it.

Billy and I now had an unspoken bond; I knew what made him tick and he in turn recognised that I saw him for what he was, a young lad too embarrassed to ask the teacher for help. That was the first time I felt an emotional connection with a pupil, and it was such a captivating moment that it reaffirmed my belief that teaching was the right career for me.

Once you've got your experience in a classroom and you've applied to your chosen course (be it through University or Schools Direct), you'll then be offered an interview. I managed to get interviews at two Schools Direct providers and a university, which I assumed gave me a fairly good chance of landing a place on a course. I thought being slightly older than your typical applicant would count in my favour and I believed I had a lot of transferable skills that would put me in good stead.

When you think about it, comedy and teaching aren't massively dissimilar jobs. At the core, both jobs require you to engage people that don't always want to be spoken to, and hold their attention for prolonged periods. Both jobs are prone to challenges of your authority, ranging from drunk middle aged men shouting out during your act to call you a "fat bald cunt", to poe-faced 11 year old children shouting out during your lesson to call you a "fat bald cunt".

My first interview was for the University course. I arrived in a smart navy blue suit, crisp white shirt, knitted tie, and polished tan leather brogues. My tactic was to treat it like a job interview and to come off professional and business focused, but also warm and approachable. Somewhere along the way this went terribly wrong and I think I came across more like a prostitute that doesn't mind being cuddled afterwards. From my recollection there were roughly a hundred candidates all interviewing for different subjects. I was going for English, the person next to me was going for French, and across from her was a chap going for Maths.

There was a palpable nervous energy in the room. Some candidates were fidgeting, others were pacing the room back and forth. I on the other hand was sitting comfortably in my chair, cool as ice. That's not because I was overly confident, rather that the years of performing on stage in front of hundreds of people every night had dulled my nerves to the point where the butterflies in my tummy had regressed back into being caterpillars.

After about 20 minutes, my name was called. I followed a young woman dressed in a mustard yellow T-shirt with the University's crest on the back. She led me up a flight of stairs and into a small space made up to look like a classroom. There was no furniture in the room, except for a long rectangular classroom table, opposite which sat three interviewees. At the other side of the table was a school chair for me to sit on.

I walked across the room and immediately felt three pairs of eyes scanning me from top to bottom, measuring my posture and gait for clues about the person that lay underneath. Almost instinctively my back straightened and my stride lengthened. My shoulders stiffened and my chest puffed out. I shook their hands in the authoritative, slightly-too-firm way that men shake hands when they're trying to appear dominant because they're secretly insecure about the size of their penis.

The interviewer on the left was an older female with glasses so thick you could fry ants with them on a warm day. She was hunched over a notepad, with a pen clutched firmly in her hand, writing notes at a furious pace. Not once throughout the entire interview did she so much as look at me, her job was purely as a scribe. The interviewer on the right was a bald gentleman with a salt-n-pepper beard that cascaded down his face like a waterfall of unruly hair. In front of him was a piece of paper, my CV, which he was studying with great intent. In between these two was a younger woman in a sharp business suit with jet black hair scraped neatly into a bun that sat slightly too high on the back of her head. She had an unnerving glare and was fixating it completely onto me, drinking in every last drop. It was she who would be asking the questions.

"So" she began in a slow, deliberate voice "let's get the standard ones out of the way. Why do you want to be a teacher?"

I'd figured this question was going to pop up. I'd thought about what I was going to say and concocted an impassioned plea about helping the disadvantaged, nurturing young minds, shaping the next generation. I must have sounded like a Miss World contestant pledging to use her powers to eradicate world hunger.

"What do you think are the three best things about being a teacher?" Instinctively I felt the stand up comedian in my try and leap out and shout "June, July and fucking August." I caught myself just in time and instead peddled out three generic, run of the mill answers about watching pupils achieve their full potential.

"Who was your favourite teacher at school and why?"

I thought about this for a long time. In the end I picked my old Maths teacher, Mr McFearlon, for the simple reason that he treated me like an adult and I respected that. It was then that the man reading my CV decided to weigh in.

"So you're a comedian, then?" His voice was derisory and I took an immediate dislike to him.

"Yes, and actually when you think about it there's a lot of transferable skills which -"

"Being a *teacher* isn't a joke, you know." He said flatly.

Being a comedian isn't a joke either" I fought back "comedians tell jokes, but I take the

business of being a comedian seriously, just like I would with teaching. And to be quite honest, I resent you implying that my job has anything to do with my professionalism or how I conduct myself."

There followed a piercing silence. Even the lady transcribing the whole affair stopped writing. Now I'm not saying I'm an expert, but when an interview feels like it's about to break into a fight then that's as sure a sign as any that it's not going particularly well.

After what felt like forever, the woman in the middle decided to pick up the baton and resume her line of inquiry. "Imagine you've got a Year 9 class and you need to pick a book for them to read. They're quite academically gifted so you'd need something to challenge them but the real issue is engaging them with the text as they don't enjoy reading. What pre-1914 fiction novel would you choose for them to read and why?"

I paused for a moment, and then out of nowhere unloaded the mother of all answers. "I'd choose The Picture of Dorian Gray, by Oscar Wilde. The reason is because it deals with themes of image obsession and perfection that are very relevant among young people today, especially with the rise in popularity of social media."

"And, just briefly, how would you go about teaching that?"

"I don't know, I haven't read it."

The interview went on for another ten minutes, but I knew at that exact moment my application was dead in the water. In case you're wondering what book a true English teacher would use, the answer is "whatever's in the fucking cupboard."

My second interview was a week later for a Schools Direct course run by my former college. This interview was run a little differently. we were asked to prepare a 20-minute lesson on a poem of our choice. I chose Emily Dickinson's "I Heard A Fly Buzz When I Died", a superb piece about the last moments of a person's life. I chose the poem mainly for its brevity - there's only four 4 line stanzas. My planning consisted of nothing more than talking about each stanza for 5 minutes apiece.

Upon arrival at the college, I was led into a spare classroom to prepare my lesson. I distinctly remember thinking "oh these poor people think I need to practice, but what they don't know is that I am a highly skilled comedian who can talk for 20 minutes without a care in the world". What "prepare your lesson" actually means is to sort out worksheets, bring up a presentation on a projector, set up any props or learning aids that you plan on using, none of which I'd considered.

After around five minutes half a dozen college pupils walked in and dotted themselves around the room, followed by three members of faculty who placed themselves at the front of the room like tweed X-factor judges. I began my lesson by talking briefly about Emily Dickinson, her background and life's work, then moving onto her distinct style and the use of hyphens synonymous with her work. I glanced at my watch, five minutes gone already. Shit, better speed things up. It was then I realised I'd made a monumental, glaring error.

There were ten of us in the room, the six people, three increasingly bewildered members of faculty, and myself. I had one copy of the poem.

I needed to keep the copy for myself seeing as I didn't have the poem memorised. I briefly considered getting everyone to crowd around the poem. In the end I just carried on, embracing the car crash rather than applying the breaks. For twenty agonising minutes I told them about a poem that none of them were allowed to see. It was, at best, the worst TED talk of all time. But I still felt confident that I could salvage something from the wreckage.

My thinking was that because it had gone badly, and I knew it had gone badly, I could win some points by analysing my mistakes and showing the interviewers that whilst I was certainly incompetent, I was by no means a living breathing Dunning-Kruger effect. Predictably during the formal interview I was asked how the lesson went, and I drilled down into my failings with the painful accuracy and deliberacy of a dentist extracting wisdom teeth.

Then came a question that completely flummoxed me - "What were the learning objectives for the lesson?"

"Learning objectives?" I asked, unsure of the terminology.

"Yes," one of the interviewers replied "what did you want them to learn?"

I had no idea. It hadn't occurred to me that it might be a good idea to think about what you want a class to come away with. I didn't know lessons had learning objectives because nobody had ever told me before. It was at this point I felt a shift from "serious interview" to "three people offering general basic advice". They gave me a few pointers for next time, rudimentary things I could do to improve, but I knew I was never going to hear back from them. Everything now rested on my third and final interview.

Last chance saloon was another Schools Direct course, this time run by a school. Their requirements were for me to do a ten minute lesson on anything I wanted, followed by a one-on-one interview afterwards. Taking stock of the last time I delivered a lesson during an interview and the disaster that ensued, I designed a short activity with a clear learning objective, accompanied by worksheets and enough copies for half the population of Luxembourg.

My ten-minute lesson revolved around spotting the poetic techniques used in the first verse of Will Smith's "Fresh Prince Of Bel-Air". There were definitions of techniques on one worksheet and the poem on another, and the idea was you had to label each time the technique had been used in the song. The activity took a little longer than ten minutes and left no time for questioning, but I got the impression the interviewers were impressed with my originality.

When the time came for my one-to-one interview I knew this was make or break. My interviewer, Paul, was an impressively forthright man. Someone who looked like he was carved out of stone, solemn and serious. He had an incredible poker face - you could just imagine him coming out of the womb with his cards clutched to his chest. Paul was not one for idle chit chat. As soon as I sat down he cut straight to what he considered to be the most pressing matter of the situation.

"I'm reading here you're a stand up comedian." He said in a low drawl. It's an unnerving thing when a person has a voice that perfectly matches their physical attributes.

"Yes," I replied firmly, "That's correct." I was anticipating another lecture about how I wasn't going to take the course seriously, but Paul had other ideas.

"My issue is that people become comedians because that's their dream in life. Why would you want to be a teacher when you're a comedian?"

I explained about the unsustainability of the live circuit as a profession that could last long term, and I spoke about the flexibility I had in terms of being able to gig at weekends and in August. This wasn't about stopping comedy, I explained, merely finding something complimentary to go alongside it. Paul seemed satisfied with the response.

"We'll have to inform the schools about it" he mused, "and I imagine there's a lot of videos and whatnot that you wouldn't want the kids to see."

"That's not a problem, I don't gig under my real name."

For the first time Paul's Easter Island Head of a face seemed to soften slightly, and a sigh of relief gushed from his cavernous mouth. The rest of the conversation was focused mainly around stand-up, and I started to think that he was beginning to see the potential in me. At the end of the interview he talked about the course and how it was structured and explained the programme in detail. He offered me a place then and there, which I accepted.

And just like that, I was in.

CHAPTER 3

The course began on the first Monday in September. I'd spent the entire of August at the Edinburgh Fringe Festival performing as part of AAA, a highly prestigious yearly showcase where promising acts are given a platform to showcase their skills at the world's largest arts festival. Our show sold out every night of the run and still lost two grand, which pretty much sums up the Fringe perfectly.

Edinburgh is a make-or-break time for a comedian. A great show can catapult you up the career ladder and open doors for TV work, tours, and the occasional deranged social media stalker.
Anything less than a great show and you leave many thousands of pounds in debt with not a lot to show for it. It's a gamble, and one that most acts feel is a necessity in order to get a leg up in the industry.

One of the comics I was house sharing with won the Perrier Award (or whatever it's now sponsored as), otherwise known as the biggest accolade in comedy. It's like winning an Oscar but instead of being surrounded by successful actors loved by millions you're surrounded by successful comics that still manage to be massive disappointments in the eyes of their parents. Another friend got spotted by one of the industry's powerhouse agencies and was immediately whisked off to Australia for three months with all expenses paid to do some festival shows and build his profile.

And here I was, in a portacabin on the outskirts of Blackburn, trying desperately not to think about how much better their careers were going.

There were nine of us on the course in total, all spread across different subjects. The tables in the room were arranged in a horseshoe and we each took a seat while we waited for Paul to arrive.

Some were chatting and exchanging general pleasantries, others like myself were more guarded, fixating themselves on their phones or rummaging around in their bags desperately trying to avoid eye contact with anyone that looked like they might want to start up a conversation.

There's a perception that comedians are outgoing and affable individuals capable of establishing a rapport with anyone. That is simply not true. The majority of comics, myself included, are incredibly socially awkward.

Paul strode into the portacabin completely unannounced, strutting like a man who'd just mastered how to walk in stilts. There was something powerful about how he carried himself - it was a

Monday morning and there were a handful of barely-awake folks in a glorified shed, and yet he came out like a champion gladiator presenting his victorious self to a crowd of Romans.

"Does anyone know the drop-out rate for a course like this?" Paul asked.

Nobody said anything. Partly because we had no idea (how could we?) but also there was a stunned silence amongst us as we wondered who in their right mind would start a course by telling us how many people wouldn't even get to the end of it.

"It's almost 50%" said Paul, not waiting for the answer to the question it was clear none of us knew. "That means between you and the person next to you, one of you won't finish the course."

We were then told, in no uncertain terms, that we could all expect to have some sort of mental breakdown between now and the end of the school year. Far be it from the 9am-3pm hours you'd expect of a school, we were told we'd be working 50-60 hour weeks. Holidays? What holidays? During half term we'd most likely be working right through trying to catch up on the work we'd missed. Sleep? No chance. Sick days? Not unless you're about to die. Time with loved ones?
Kiss it the fuck goodbye my friend. If you even so much as stop to

have a wank, you best be marking papers with your free hand. Paul's tigerish approach worked with some people, but not with me. Rather than taking a moment for introspection and asking myself whether I *really* wanted to do this and if I was prepared for the monumental level of effort and commitment required of me, I spent about fifteen minutes studying each of my course mates individually trying to work out who I thought was going to be the first to jack it in. Sort of like a bizarre teaching Deadpool, if you will.

The rest of the day was spent getting to know my fellow course mates. Paul was keen to stress the value of having a support network so that when times became difficult we'd have people to talk to who were going through a shared experience. We each took it in turns to tell the group our names, where we were from, what subject we were going to be teaching, and what our job background was.

First to introduce herself was Andrea. Coming from Wigan, she was in her mid 40s and had a face that could stand clogging. Andrea was no stranger to the classroom, she'd worked as a teaching assistant for the last ten years and that experience had instilled a cocky confidence in her that I took an immediate dislike to. Her subject specialism was History, something we later found out she had no actual qualifications in.

Next was Tony, a giant bear of a man with curly black locks who looked like what would happen if you crossed Gaston with Shrek. He was taking P.E, no surprises there, from the sheer size of him he'd struggle to fit in a classroom. Following him were Zach, a good looking man in his mid 20s, and Linda, a mousy woman from Chorley, both taking Science.

Charlene, a bubbly woman specialising in Religious Education whom I guessed to be in her 40s, spent five times longer than anyone else introducing herself, words falling out of her face in a nervous excitement. She also happened to have the biggest arse I've ever seen on any human being. It was like listening to a centaur in a dress. Anna on the other hand was incredibly professional and forthright, dressed sharply in the most corporate of business attire she managed to sum up her entire life in about ten words. Her subject was Maths.

Beside Anna sat Chelsea, a blonde young thing in her early 20s with impeccable makeup and a chatty disarming demeanour. She was going to be teaching Science. The woman next to me stood up, Saima, an Asian girl fresh out of University. She was taking English. Finally, it was my turn to tell the group my story.

If there's one thing I hate it's telling people that I'm a comedian. It's an unusual vocation, so it's common for people to take a sudden interest in you and bombard you with questions. I'm sure there's no malice behind it - rather I think we've become so used to asking people what they do for a living and pretending to give a shit about the answer, that when someone has a genuinely fascinating job we interrogate them ferociously.

That wouldn't be too much of a problem, but people ALWAYS ask the same questions. Are you funny? Yes dick head, it's sort of like a prerequisite for the job. Do you know (insert famous comedian's name)? Someone once asked me if I knew who Michael McIntyre was. You know, one of the most famous comedians in the world. So for a laugh I said no, thinking they'd realise I was taking the piss. Sadly not, they then spent half an hour reciting his jokes to me while I mentally listed all the things in the room I could kill myself with. And last but not least, the dreaded one, "tell me a joke". Only with comedians do we have to prove our job to you. If I told you I was an electrician you wouldn't ask me to re-wire a plug to see whether or not I was any good.

The other issue is that when people realise I'm a comedian, they have an expectation that I'm going to spontaneously make them laugh. As previously stated, I'm quite socially awkward, so when people hear I'm a stand up there's this weird moment where they wait for me to do or say something inherently hilarious, and I'm waiting for them to dictate the conversation, and neither of us does what the other's hoping for so we just kind of stare at each other for an awkward few minutes and they go away assuming I'm shit.

Now I've been a comedian for over ten years, during which I've been introduced to strangers thousands of times. I've therefore picked up a couple of tricks to avoid having the awkward conversation. Whenever someone asks me what I do for a living, I tell them that I'm self-employed. This usually stops the conversation dead most of the time. Occasionally you'll get someone who presses further and asks "doing what?" And my answer is just to tell them that I own my own business. The vast majority of the time people move on and decide I'm a little cagey and secretive, which is wildly preferable to them thinking you're a dreadful and deluded stand up.

"Hello, I'm Freddy" I stated, standing up to address the group, "I'm self employed and I'm going to be teaching English." I motioned to sit back down however across the other end of the room
came a question.

"Doing what?" asked Andrea.

"Oh, I've got my own business."

"What's your business then?" Andrea pressed, as though I was in the witness box and she were

some high powered lawyer tasked with getting the truth, the whole truth and nothing but the truth out of me.

"I, erm, well…." from the far side of the room I could see Paul paying close attention to how I navigated this, so I decided to approach it head on. "Well I'm actually a stand up comedian."

"No way!" Andrea exclaimed, her booming Wigan voice filling the room like a megaphone in a phone box, "are you funny?"

"Well, I try to be."

"Have you heard of, erm, what's his name, that posh guy with the weird laugh?"

"Jimmy Carr?"

"Yes! Oh I love him. I saw him last year with my friend and her husband. Are you as good as Jimmy Carr?"

"Well right now he's a multimillionaire with millions of fans and I'm talking to you in a room with no central heating and a corrugated iron roof, so I'd probably say no."

The rest of my course mates had their own questions too, and I awkwardly tried to answer as many as I could. Sensing my exhaustion, Paul stepped in. "While we're on the subject, it's important not to divulge your or anyone else's personal lives to the pupils. And while you're at it, make sure you change all your social media accounts to private."

We took a short break for lunch and conversation turned to our bursaries. You see, in order to encourage more people to become teachers, the government will pay a monthly grant to those doing a QTS course. This, in theory, is a great idea designed at removing the financial obstacles behind spending a year training for free. However, not all prospective teachers are paid the same fee. Some aren't paid a fee at all. It all comes down to whether or not the government decides your subject specialism is in demand or not.

As an English teacher, my bursary was £400 per month. This was barely enough to cover my rent and bills, and certainly not enough to cover food and travel. Luckily the majority of a comedian's work comes at weekends, so I'd be able to earn enough money to get by. If you're a Science teacher your monthly bursary is £1000. Anna, the maths teacher, somewhat begrudgingly revealed she was receiving £2000 a month. The face on P.E teacher Tony was one of sheer disbelief - he was getting nothing.

Upon overhearing us discussing our finances, Paul informed us that for anyone wanting to teach Physics the bursary was £3000. That's the equivalent to the take home pay of a £47,500 a year job. Once a Physics teacher actually gets a job in teaching, they were effectively taking a 50% pay cut. Paul further disclosed that there'd been a recent spate of physics graduates taking up roles on teacher courses, not because they had any innate desire to actually *become* a teacher, but because it was just about the best paying graduate job out there. Once they qualified as a teacher, instead of moving into the profession, they simply left and went onto other things.

I was starting to see why half the people on the course dropped out. The bursary conversation was a sore subject with many, and I was personally incredulous that Anna was being paid five times more than me for doing the same thing. Later on I spoke with Tony, who told me that had he been aware of the fact that everyone was getting a bursary but him, he'd have never gone on the course in the first place. I could see him weighing up whether or not to throw in the towel there and then as a defiant act of protest.

Mentally, I put Tony's name at the top of my Deadpool.

It only took two or three days of icebreaker activities for the novelty of being on a new course to wear off. Slowly but surely the carefully polished, flawless veneers we'd all painstakingly crafted to make us appear perfect began to chip away and expose the uglier aspects of our personality. Zach started arriving late. "Traffic" he'd say, as if there was no way of possibly predicting that a road might have other cars on it. Chelsea began to glance at her phone in-between activities. I'd even lost my cool once during an activity called "Pack Types" where we had to pick cards with certain attributes that we felt best mirrored our personality, only to flip the card over and see what sort of dog breed we were. "This is fucking pointless" I said, feeling somewhat irked at having to wake up at 7am to play what looked like Happy Families crossed with Crufts.

By the time Friday came around there was a palpable sense of relief between us. Paul had told us that next week we would be placed in the secondary schools which we would attend until Christmas. This would be known as "Placement One". After the Christmas half term, we would then be assigned at a different school where we would remain until the end of the course.

Somewhat predictably, they called this "Placement Two".

Paul produced a stack of plastic wallets with our names on a sticker label in the upper right hand corner. Stuffed inside the wallets were papers full of information about our first placement, including the location of the school, the names of the members of the faculty we'd be working alongside and names of SLT (Senior Leadership Team, basically the Headteacher, Deputy Heads, and anyone else vitally important to be on your best behaviour around).

As soon as my wallet hit the desk in front of me I began rifling through its contents trying to absorb every drop of information about my first placement. The school was called "Moorfields High School" and I was going to be spending the next three months there with Saima and, joy of joys, Andrea. The school catered for just over a thousand pupils and was rated "Good" by OFSTED.

OFSTED, by the way, is the regulatory body in charge of classifying every educational institute in the country. Their very name sends a chill up the spine of even the most battle-hardened teacher. They can call at any time and show up at your front door at 8am the next day, delving into every aspect of the school - from teachers to cleaners, extra-curricular activities to safeguarding, budgets and finances to job performances - nothing escapes their relentless burrowing in search of the truth.

Everybody knows that schools are never perfect. There's always a toilet that needs fixing or a
fence that needs securing, and a pupil (more often more than one) that we've run out of ideas to help, and a teacher struggling, and a department failing, and exams and books that need marking.
You are in a state of perpetual catch up. So when you get that call from OFSTED, every single one of those issues needs sorting within 24 hours. It's not uncommon for teachers to pull all-nighters, staying till the early hours of the morning trying to get the school in the best possible shape for the impending inspection.

Because what OFSTED has to say about your school matters. A lot.

There are four grades OFSTED can give a school - Outstanding, Good, Requires Improvement and Inadequate. There's a common misconception amongst the general public that an Outstanding school is some middle-class countryside grammar school where they learn Latin and play Polo, and an Inadequate school is some inner-city faux ghetto where gang-coloured durags are part of the uniform. This is just not true; you can have fancy schools with clever pupils that are run appallingly, and you can have urban schools with less academically capable and more socio-economically disadvantaged pupils that provide the best possible learning environments. Nor is it about the standard of teaching; there are incredible teachers working in god-awful schools and there are dreadful teachers working in some of the most respected establishments in the country.

If your school is rated as Outstanding or Good, OFSTED generally leave you alone. They might check in once every 5 years to see how things are going, it's usually a short visit. However once your school hits Requires Improvement or Inadequate that's when things become more complicated. The regularity of visits increases, recommendations are made and if not properly followed people lose jobs.

Once a school is downgraded and becomes Requires Improvement or Inadequate, the reaction of the SLT (Senior Leadership Team) is usually to implement wholesale and drastic school-wide changes to 'stop the rot'. More often than not, such changes are downright unmanageable and

triple the workload of already overworked teachers to the point where it's even harder to perform to a high standard because there's less time to do more things.

A typical example of this can be found in this story about a friend of mine whose school was downgraded from Good to Requires

Improvement. One of the issues OFSTED highlighted was inconsistent and inconsequential marking. The school's reaction was to introduce a new marking policy whereby teachers had to use five different coloured pens when marking work. This meant that every piece of work effectively had to be marked five times over, causing a massive backlog of work as staff struggled to keep up. When OFSTED returned they found the marking in a
worse condition than when they left.

A poor OFSTED report has consequences far beyond the realms of the classroom. Parents do not want to send their little darlings to a school that's been classed as Inadequate, and rightly so.
Education is one of the most important aspects of a child's life, and everyone wants what's best for their kids. I mean, you wouldn't have an operation at a hospital that the NHS described as Inadequate, would you?

If parents are more reluctant to send their kids to your school then the intake of pupils will decrease. When that happens so too does the money you get from the government. If a school built to house 1000 children suddenly only has 800 then funding becomes an issue. Staff will be made redundant. Departments will have to be prioritised over others. Purse strings will be tightened and staff will be asked to do more with less. And it comes as no surprise that, when a school is failing, giving them even *less* money usually exacerbates the downward spiral.

It's a slippery slope from which the road to recovery can take many years. There are some pupils who'll join a "Good" school in Year 7 and have OFSTED come in later only to rate it "Inadequate". Then while the school spends the next five years trying to get back to their previous rating while you prepare to sit your GCSEs at a school that's been deemed unfit for

purpose the entire time you've been there. Unless you've got the money to take your child out of state education completely and pay for a private school.

CHAPTER 4

As a child your first day at secondary school is like the first time you try coffee - your heart beats faster, you're jittery and on edge, and if you're particularly unfortunate you just might shit your pants. For a start, it's much larger than the primary school you've known your whole life.

Everything is new; the buildings, the uniform, the teachers. There are so many things to remember. When you're in Year 6 you have one teacher and one classroom. A year later there's dozens of them. You go from being the biggest kids in school to the smallest. You're thrown in with children from other schools, most of whom you don't know, so there's the pressure of having to establish yourself all over again. The only solace is that you're not alone. In fact, everyone in your year group is going through more or less the same thing.

For that reason teaching a Year 7 class in September is a wondrous experience. They arrive at the school so eager to please that they are terrified of doing anything wrong. Many of these children have formed an intense bond with their teacher every year, in fact outside of their own parents their teacher is probably the adult that spends the most time with them. And so they arrive at secondary school *desperate* for you to like them.

The pressure they bestow upon themselves for your approval means that quite often they will behave in the most unusual of ways. For starters, they will ask questions about EVERY. SINGLE. THING.

"What's the title?"

"Where do we write the title?"

"Should we underline the title?"

"Where should we write the date?"

"What was the title again?" "Should I use a pen or pencil?"

"Can I use a pen for the title and pencil to underline?"

"Where does the date go?"

"Do we write the month and year?"

"Should I underline with a ruler?"

"Where does the date go?"

"What's the title?"

Before you know it, twenty minutes of the lesson has gone. I had one new Year 7 put her hand up once to tell me she'd finished her page and wanted to know whether or not she should turn the page over and continue writing on the other side of the paper. As opposed to what, writing on the table? Continuing from the table onto her leg and torso? Carrying on until her whole body is covered with writing like she's in Memento? Jesus Christ Charlotte, of course you write on the next page.

It's easy to let your frustrations get the better of you when thirty kids are each asking ten questions a lesson, like a bizarre hour long game of Mastermind where the specialist subject is "information I've already told you". But for the first couple of months the Year 7s are so vulnerable that most of the time is spent being extra nice to them so they don't explode into tears. Most schools have a network of staff tasked with helping the transition from primary to secondary; usually consisting of the Head of Year 7, the form tutors, and the pastoral staff. Between them meetings are held on a regular basis to try and identify children who are finding their new surroundings especially difficult.

Sometimes you can see the ones having trouble adjusting from miles away. A common way of spotting those who are struggling is through watching out for poor behaviour. Children can often feel as though they don't get the same level of attention at secondary school, and some seek to make up the shortfall in other ways. In their minds, attention for being naughty is better than no attention at all. For other students, attendance is the issue. They avoid school like an anti-vaxxer denying logic and reason, and the only thing this accomplishes is to make the process of assimilation all the harder.

It didn't take long for me to find a Year 7 in floods of tears, hiding underneath the stairs like a shit Harry Potter. The poor thing let out uncontrollable sobs, big fat tears that seemed to crash to the ground and form salty puddles around her feet. She was so inconsolable that when I found her, my initial reaction was that something terrible must have happened. Was she in pain? Did a loved one die? As it turned out, the reason for her cries of anguish was much less of a big deal than her emotions would have you believe. "I've…I've… I've forgotten my pen!" She said, erupting once more into a fit of hysterics.

I spent several minutes calming her down and reassuring her that it really wasn't a big deal. I briefly considered telling her that skipping class however was far more serious, but thought better of it. If this is how she reacted to forgetting a piece of stationary, realising she was currently AWOL would have likely tipped her into a full blown meltdown.

"Are they going to expel me?" She spluttered through handfuls of tears. I let out an involuntary chuckle that caught her off guard. Perhaps she thought I was here to take her away and send her off to a specialist housing for unruly children who commit the heinous crime of not having something to write with.

"No, of course not." I reassured her. "Here, you can have mine." I said, giving her an old biro from my pocket. She looked at me like I'd just given her a kidney. "What lesson are you meant to be in now?"

"French, with Mr Pike" she replied, with a quiver in her voice that told me she hadn't fully calmed down.

"Well why don't we go there together now and I'll tell Mr Pike you got lost, and we can keep the pen thing a secret just between us - can I ask what your name is?"

"It's Milly."

"Well Milly, I'd guard that pen like your life depended on it." I said, with a tongue-in-cheeky

tone designed to let her know that it really wasn't important and not worth worrying about. And with that, she darted off to her lesson, moving with the freedom of someone who's just had the weight of the world lifted off her shoulders.

This kind of empathy came naturally to me. I was in a new environment too and there was no doubt I was sharing the same anxieties as the children navigating their first few days. As a trainee teacher, from the moment you park your car to the minute you drive away, you are being watched. Staff are trying to size you up and work out what kind of person they're going to be dealing with. They pick up on every infraction. Did you check your phone during that meeting? Someone saw you. Did you sneak away for a cigarette at break time? Someone saw you. Did you arrive a couple of minutes late? Someone saw you. And they're making notes.

When you're new you try really hard to impress your colleagues and peers to earn their respect.

The best way to do this is to appear competent, don't put a foot wrong. But not making any mistakes as a trainee teacher is literally impossible. You will make thousands. Most of the time, you're not even aware you're making a mistake until someone points it out to you. For the first two months at Moorfields I was accidentally parking in the assistant head's parking space. It wasn't marked or anything official, it's just this guy has worked at the school for nearly two decades and always parked in that space and everyone just *knew* that was his spot. I only found out when my Head of Department pulled me to one side, asked what my car registration was and then very politely but very firmly told me to park on the residential road opposite the school from now on.

On the first day at Moorfields myself, Saima and Andrea met our Course Leader, a woman called Margaret. She was a charming woman with a wide, sincere smile that spread generously between her plump cherry red cheeks. A bob of graying blonde hair sat atop her head, below which small beady eyes nestled gently on her face. Margaret told us a little about herself and her background; she'd attended Moorfields as a pupil before getting her teaching qualification and coming straight back, and had been teaching here ever since.

There didn't seem to be anything particularly remarkable about Margaret, that is until you watched her in the classroom. She exuded calmness, her aura was one of complete and total control. She didn't so much as deal with classroom disruption as anticipate it and neutralise the situation before it even had a chance to develop. I read once that the best football defenders often make fewer tackles than their counterparts because they are better at intercepting the ball. They read the game so well that they don't need to tackle, they have stopped the attack before it's even had a chance to develop. In that sense, Margaret was some sort of educational Paolo Maldini, gliding around the classroom with swan-like grace, intercepting potential problems by thinking three steps ahead.

After spending her whole life teaching, her awareness was astonishing. It was a finely honed sixth sense. A kid would be rooting in his bag looking for a pen and by the time he'd popped his head up there'd already be one on his desk. Before a child could even finish writing a note to his friend, she'd taken the note off him, binned it, and replaced it with a handwritten detention slip. I didn't think much of Margaret when I first saw her, but by the end of the day I was in awe of her. We all were. It takes a lifetime of dedication to make something as tricky as teaching look so effortless.

As the Course Leader, Margaret was responsible for looking after us and guiding us through our first placement. She would do her best to sort out problems we might be having, but the flip side of that is that if we were causing problems ourselves she'd be the one with her foot up our arse. Alongside Margaret we'd each have our own personal mentor who'd be our first point of contact and the person we'd be working most closely with.

Margaret was explaining all this whilst at the same time showing us around the school, never once tripping over her words or repeating herself. She explained two things at once like it was the most normal, natural thing in the world. Even just walking around the school with Margaret was an experience. Over her 40-odd years she'd gotten to know every single nook and cranny, knew everything about each member of staff who all knew her in return and shot respectful, admiring comments and small talk in her direction. It was like a scene in some mafia film where a don shows you around their neighborhood and all the residents stop what they're doing and bow in complete deference.

Once the tour was completed Margaret led us into the staff room and announced that we would shortly be introduced to our personal mentors. These would be people who were our first point of contact in the school. They'd be showing us the ropes and guiding us appropriately.

What I didn't know at the time is that your relationship with your mentor is quite possibly the single most important aspect of a school placement. A good mentor will make life a thousand times easier in every conceivable way; they'll have your back, clean up after your mistakes, and pick you up on the many occasions where you feel completely broken and beaten. Conversely, a bad mentor is about as useful as a shit in a swimming pool. Forging a strong relationship between you and your mentor is quite often the difference between passing and dropping out.

Andrea's mentor came in first, a stone cold woman in her late thirties with piercing eyes and suspicious lips that looked like they hadn't seen joy in years. After the briefest of introductions Andrea was whisked off to the History department. Two more mentors for Saima and I followed shortly afterwards. Saima's mentor Kat was a single mother who had moved to this school the year before. My mentor was younger than me, early to mid 20s and in her second year of teaching, also known as an RQT (Recently Qualified Teacher).

The first thing I noticed about my new mentor was how jaw-droppingly beautiful she was. Her eyes were wide and soft, her blonde curly hair suited her slender frame perfectly, her voice was smooth and luscious and, perhaps most strikingly, she seemed to radiate a natural warmth given off by her effortless charm. Her name was Holly. I fancied her immediately. But I needn't have worried about anything developing between us; for one she was engaged, secondly I was in a happy and stable long term relationship and thirdly, and perhaps most pertinently, she was so far out of my league we probably weren't even playing the same sport. Being in a couple with her would be like watching Scarlett Johansson driving a Fiat Cinquecento, you'd be far more inclined to think she was doing it for a bet than that she actually liked the car.

A large part of whether or not you and your mentor will gel together is dependent on your personalities. Holly and I both loved to gossip, so we had an instant and natural rapport with one another. Both Kat and Saima were more clinical and businessman-like, they appreciated efficiency and working smart was tantamount to success. They also formed a strong bond right away. Andrea, on the other hand, despised her mentor.

In our first week we were asked to deliver a "starter" for a lesson. Much like in the world of culinary fine dining, a starter is something that primes you for what is about to come. It wets your appetite, gets you ready for the main course. With very few exceptions, it is conventional teaching wisdom that each lesson must begin with a starter. Side note, if you're reading this years from now and starters are no longer used in teaching, this is because "conventional teaching wisdom" is cyclical and changes every few years. When I last taught a class there was a big push on "growth mindset" whatever the fuck that is. A few years before that it was all about learning styles and whether you're a kinesthetic learner or an auric learner. Christ knows what it'll be next but whatever they come up with one thing's for certain, Assistant Head Teachers will make a big song and dance about how it'll revolutionise learning whilst old school teachers who've been around the block a few times will sit in the back of meetings rolling their eyes at this new repackaged bullshit.

Starters come in a range of different shapes and sizes. They might recap the last lesson or introduce a new topic. They might be in the form of a discussion with your partner, or a time to reflect quietly on your own. Whatever form they take, they should be approximately ten minutes long, be engaging enough to garner interest, and should be what we call "low floor, high ceiling"
- teacher language for "really easy to contribute *something*, but with enough challenge that the more academically able pupils are able to push themselves into contributing something more difficult."

We were given roughly two days' warning that we should prepare a starter, which in the world of teaching is an eternity and then some. Holly's advice to me was to keep it simple. You might think ten minutes is an awfully long time, but by the time they've all sat down, you've taken the register, they've got their books and pens out, one kid's lost his book, two more are asking to borrow a pen, one comes in late and you have to mark them on the register, before you know it you've lost a significant chunk of the lesson already.

The day before we were due to deliver for the first time in front of a class, Saima, Andrea and I were in the staff room preparing. Saima seemed fairly apprehensive and this was manifesting itself in giddy excitement. She seemed to be relishing the prospect. I adopted my trademark laid back state, my brain figuring that ten minutes in front of some Year 8s couldn't ever be anywhere near as bad as last week's thirty minute set in front of 250 pissed up Liverpudlians. Andrea, on the other hand, was nothing short of a wreck. Frantically cutting out hundreds of bits of paper, completely incredulous at my lack of worry.

Saima asked politely whether we could help and shot a stern glance in my direction that indicated in no uncertain terms that I should also be offering. I asked her what she was planning for her starter, and she replied with the most contrived activity I think I've ever heard in my life. It all revolved around posters around the room which had facts about Henry VIII. Each pupil had three cards, red, yellow and green and they were going to be given 60 seconds to stick cards over the facts in question. A red card meant the fact was untrue, a green card meant it was true and a yellow card meant they were unsure.

"That sounds a bit complicated, doesn't it?" I enquired, mindful of how my mentor had advised simplicity was the key.

Angela immediately became defensive. "No, ACTUALLY. I've seen this work *loads of times* in my old school and ACTUALLY a lot of teachers here probably use it too so ACTUALLY it's a great way to introduce yourself to a class. What are you going to do anyway?"

I told her I'd picked two characters from the book we were reading and had a list of adjectives. Pupils had to decide, in pairs, which adjective best suited which character. Andrea heard this and snorted as though it were the most inane idea in the history of the universe "Trust me, hon, they'll have finished that in like two minutes."

The following afternoon myself and Saima were sitting back in the staff room discussing our starter activities. Both had exceeded our expectations and we were remarking over how good it felt to get your first lesson under your belt, so to speak. Andrea entered the room with a stack of green, yellow and red cards under her arm. She looked crestfallen. Apparently her starter had not gone according to plan, and that's putting it mildly. A better description might well be "complete fucking unmitigated disaster."

Andrea began explaining the event and it sounded as though anything and everything that could have gone wrong did go wrong. To start with, Andrea had given every child a piece of blu-tack to stick their cards to the poster with. Unfortunately kids and blu-tack are a potent mix, and they promptly began sticking cards on each other instead. The cards themselves were too big and once one pupil had stuck a card over a fact nobody else could read it, so other pupils began removing cards to see what the facts were underneath. Also the facts were far too difficult, as Henry VIII was a new topic none of them knew much about him. This total shitshow, advertised length ten minutes, ended up being THIRTY minutes long. Even then that's because her mentor, slowly watching the car crash unfold before her very eyes, stepped in and relieved Andrea of her duties in the hopes of salvaging something from the lesson.

It was hard not to feel smug about the whole thing. Our lessons, which she'd been so dismissive of, were a roaring success while hers fell flat on its arse. I was just picking the perfect moment to say

"ACTUALLY" half a dozen times right in her face when I noticed she was crying. Clearly she'd felt utterly humiliated by it all. She'd been talking a big game since day one and now she'd fallen at the first hurdle. We both began to console her. I still didn't like her, but it just seemed like the human thing to do.

Andrea's introspective moment of self-reflection was fleeting. Within five minutes she'd decided that how her mentor had conducted herself was completely unprofessional and compromised her integrity in front of the rest of the class. Saima tried reasoning with her but was told that "ACTUALLY how the children perceive you is very important and ACTUALLY is probably the reason why the activity didn't work." So it wasn't because of the cards, or the facts being too hard, or it taking half the lesson. No, the reason Andrea failed to dazzle is because the pupils must have somehow picked up on her mentor's scepticism.

At the end of the day we all had a meeting with our mentors and the course leader Margaret to discuss how our starter activities went. The meeting began in a gentile fashion, pleasantries were exchanged, and both Saima and I were given faint praise for our lesson starters. I glanced over to Andrea who was grinding her teeth as though she'd just slipped three pills at an illegal rave.

"Andrea, yours didn't go so well, why was that?" Asked Margaret. "Well, I just feel like my mentor completely undermined me." The table was aghast. Andrea's mentor's mouth was open as far as mouths can go, practically hanging off her jaw.

"What do you mean by that?" Margaret inquired. Her delivery was purposeful. She knew she was walking in a field surrounded by emotional landmines.

"Well she cut my lesson short and that completely undermined me in front of the whole class and it's not how you should treat me as a colleague."

"But the thing is," Margaret replied, choosing her words carefully before delivering the sucker punch, "we aren't colleagues."

Andrea was dumbfounded.
She continued. "You might think we are, but we're not. We don't have the same responsibilities, do we? If that class doesn't get their GCSE target grades, none of the parents are going to call you, are they? The head isn't going to drag you into the office and demand answers. When you make a mistake, we are the ones that have to pick up the pieces. Now I suggest you go home and you think about your approach to this course, and maybe come back with a bit of humility.

Because if you start thinking you're colleagues with someone when you've not been here a week then it's not going to work going forward."

If you've ever seen a grown adult tell another adult off, it's quite an unnerving sight to behold, and I had front seat tickets. Andrea, all bluster just moments ago, had been reduced to total silence by the power of Margaret's words and her unforgiving frankness.

Although we were still early on in the course, Andrea had exposed her biggest weakness. She was completely unable to take any form of criticism. She needed to be told again and again how wonderful she was. Sadly this is not the course for molly-coddling and even if it were, her mentor looked like she was allergic to compliments. Especially when Andrea tried calling her out in front of everyone. Silently I watched the drama unfold in front of me, and mentally placed Andrea's name at the top of the Deadpool.

As I left the meeting I noticed Milly was in the room opposite having a detention. Turns out a boy in her class had stolen the pen I'd given her so in retaliation she'd kicked him square in the balls with enough ferocity to delay puberty by about 18 months. Sounds like she took the "guard you pen like your life depends on it" advice a little too literally.

CHAPTER 5

Over the coming weeks we gradually settled into life at Moorfields and became accustomed to its rhythm. The 'rhythm' of a school is a weird alchemy made up of many ingredients; the length of lessons, involvement from SLT, faculty meetings, after school clubs, engagement in sporting activities, behavioral procedures, lunchtime and break protocols, curriculum, extra-curricular activities, chemistry with other staff, and millions of other little components all play a part in giving every school a unique 'feel'. Settling well into the rhythm of a school is vital when it comes to being happy there.

Every high school in the country does things slightly differently. These minute variations can add up to huge wholesale changes on how education is managed. What one school considers sacrosanct another just down the road might see as a pointless endeavour. When absorbing yourself in a new school, the key is to be flexible in your approach. If you walk into a new school and judge it by the standards of your old one, you're going to find it extremely hard to fit into their way of operating.

At Moorfields there were five hour-long lessons each day. School began with fifteen minutes for form time, after which there would be two lessons, then a break, followed by two more lessons, then lunch, then one final lesson after which the bell would ring and children would scurry out in all directions like rats leaving a sinking ship. Some children may stay behind for detention or after school clubs, but by and large most sprinted out of the place as though their lives depended on it.

There is a common misconception amongst those who don't work in education that schools finish at 3pm and the teachers leave at quarter past. Let me set the record straight - that is a pile of festering horse shit so high you'd need a team of Sherpas to climb it. The overwhelming majority of teachers clock in before 8am and leave after 5pm. All of them take work home to do on weekends. The job demands your devotion. At Moorfields we were told within our first week that, even though school finished at 3pm, we shouldn't be leaving before 4pm without an exceptionally good reason.

Another thing one quickly comes to realise is that breaks and lunches are far from the personal moments of solitude and serenity you'd hope for them to be. Once or twice a week you will have to be a "monitor", which basically consists of being a sentinel garrisoned somewhere within the playground, toilets or lunch hall, tasked with keeping a vigilant eye on the children to stop them breaking things and generally kicking the shit out of each other.

Depending on where you are put, being a monitor can be anything from a slight irritation to a massive pain in the arse. The best place you can be is guarding a hallway or an entrance. It's a really easy job, you basically just tell kids to piss off for fifteen minutes. So much so that some teachers spend their breaks finding new and creative ways to tell children to piss off when they ask to come inside.

"Are you in need of urgent medical attention?" Mrs Mason, head of Science would ask.

"No, but…."

"Do you suppose, to the best of your estimations, that you are in danger of dropping dead within the next ten to fifteen minutes?"

The child would at this point be rendered silent, wondering what the hell was happening.

"Well then, I would propose there's no need for you to go inside, is there? If you are going to die you can do so in your next lesson."

The worst place to be positioned was undoubtedly the toilets. Pupils would stay there all lunch if they could. They'd much rather eat their packed lunch over a toilet bowl surrounded by fecal matter than in an actual dining room. It boggles the mind. The reason it's such a pain to have to guard the loos is because every pupil is smart enough to know you're not supposed to be in there, and they also know you're limited to what sort of questions you can ask them without coming across as the world's biggest pervert.

One time whilst stuck on toilet duty I attempted Mrs Mason's over-the-top brash approach. A Year 9 girl tried accessing the toilet two minutes before break was over (a school no-no) and I took this as the perfect chance to test out my new persona of sarcastic disciplinarian.

"Are you in urgent need of the toilet? Do you suppose, to the best of your estimations, that you are in danger of leaking within the next ten to fifteen minutes?" I asked.

"Well, I'm on my period, so yeah."
That was the last time I tried to be like Mrs Mason. I certainly wasn't brave enough to tell a teenage girl "If you're going to bleed you can do so in your next lesson."

By the time October half term rolled round we were all suitably knackered but in relatively high spirits. At one course meeting one or two of us even exchanged cautiously optimistic sentiments about how this was far from the grueling slog we'd been told to brace ourselves for and was actually *easier* than one was expecting. How naive we were. The marathon that is the teacher training course does not take place on flat ground. There are some bits that are easier than others; some stages can be cruised through at a leisurely pace, whereas other stages are an uphill struggle where every step, every breath, feels like a herculean struggle.

Indeed, one of the first lessons young prospective teachers learn is that of being able to prioritise what's most important. Fairly quickly in your career you realise there are just not enough hours in the day to do every single thing asked of you, and that some jobs have to take priority over others. Tasks such as marking and lesson planning are a constant burden and will always be at the forefront of your mind whereas implementing a new seating plan for your set three Year 9's because Lucy and Hannah have fallen out and don't want to sit next to each other isn't exactly high up on your pecking order.

The time of a teacher is precious, and yet constantly overloaded with a bizarre menagerie of aimless duties. Most of the time from the start of school till the end is taken delivering lessons; out of a timetable of 5 lessons a day for 5 days a week, within those 25 periods a teacher may only have one or two periods free. The rest of the time, you're teaching classes. On top of that, each lesson needs to be thoroughly planned, resources need to be created and prepared, slideshows and presentations must be constructed. Then there's marking classwork and homework. Then there's after school engagements; running social clubs, parents evenings, staff meetings, departmental evaluations, training days, detentions. Then there's the pupils themselves - does someone in your class need extra support? Is someone in your form being bullied? Has someone got issues at home? Are there safeguarding concerns?

There are simply not enough hours in the day to do all of these things, let alone to do them well. And just when you think you're at your capacity, that there's simply no more time left and that every free second of your life has been wrung dry from your withered body, the government will occasionally announce a wholesale change to education and throw your life into unmitigated chaos at the drop of a hat.

Naturally trainee teachers aren't exposed to all of these demands straight away, in much the same way that opticians advise against staring at the sun without eye protection. Instead, you are given small incremental doses of your responsibilities, kind of like how doctors make a body develop immunity to a virus. They give you a tiny dose, they see if you can handle it, they give you a little bit more, check again to see how you're doing, then give you a bit more and they keep going until you've taken the lot.

Here we were, having been given the smallest of doses, thinking we were immortal. We were about to find out just how wrong we were.

CHAPTER 6

After the October half term our course leader Paul called us all in for a meeting. This was the first time we'd seen each other in person since the opening week of the Schools Direct programmed and, aside from a few slightly disheveled faces, nobody had thrown in the towel just yet. It was clear, however, that some were finding it more difficult than others. Charlene, a

trainee in Religious Education (or Religious Studies depending on what your school prefers to call the one hour a week you sit and learn about God) told us she'd spent most nights up until 2am getting ready for the following day. Anna, the industrious Maths teacher, had quietly revealed she'd been spending the October half term planning out lessons from now up until

Christmas in a calculated attempt to manage her work load. I remember feeling more than a little foolish telling her I'd essentially had two weeks off, and hadn't even *thought* about teaching.

Paul prowled around the room like a tiger, handing us each a sizable A4 book. "These" he said "are your Records Of Achievement. There are 8 teaching criterias we focus on and you need to attain a "good" or "outstanding" grade in each criteria in order to pass this course. You need to collect evidence of each piece of criteria being met, and you'll keep these in your evidence folders." He then began handing out plastic folders to go along with our new books.

We were given a moment to read through the eight teaching standards we had been presented with;

1. Set high expectations which inspire, motivate and challenge pupils.

2. Promote good progress and outcomes by pupils.

3. Demonstrate good subject and curriculum knowledge.

4. Plan and teach well-structured lessons.

5. Adapt teaching to respond to the strengths and needs of all pupils.

6. Make accurate and productive use of assessment.

7. Manage behaviour effectively to ensure a good and safe

learning environment.
8. Fulfil wider professional responsibilities.

Each standard was broken down into further criteria that needed to be met. For example, the subsections for standard 6 were as follows;

- know and understand how to assess the relevant subject and curriculum areas, including statutory assessment requirements.

- make use of formative and summative assessment to secure pupils' progress.

- use relevant data to monitor progress, set targets, and plan subsequent lessons.

- give pupils regular feedback, both orally and through accurate marking, and encourage pupils to respond to the feedback.

My head spun. Between the 8 teaching standards and the numerous sections they were divided into, there were approximately 50 criteria that needed to be met and fully evidenced.
Furthermore, each criteria was broken down even more by having

three "grades" associated with how well you've met them. The myriad of choices was dizzying.

I started to think about how I could even show evidence for some of these. I mean, what piece of paper did I need to photocopy that would show that I have managed to "establish a safe and stimulating environment for pupils, rooted in mutual respect"? Perhaps I could record some of my class swearing on a bible that I've never punched them in the face? Maybe some sort of elaborate polygraph test?

Paul then produced some evidence folders from previous courses so we could see the kind of thing previous graduates had used. They were enormous; bursting at the seams with coloured stickers and plastic wallets and fancy dividers. It was a real treasure to behold - even though to look at one you didn't specifically understand all of its contents, you got a real sense that this was a labour of love. Someone had put blood, sweat and tears into this and, for a few short months at least, their entire lives revolved around its completion. As if the magnitude of these vast bibles may have been lost upon us, Paul reiterated their significance. "If you do not complete your evidence folder, you cannot be awarded a teaching qualification."

Our lives at Moorfields changed as soon as we came back, evidence folders tucked under our arms. No longer was it acceptable to just turn up to a lesson, be vaguely entertaining, and hope that some learning materialised from it - from now on every single one of our lessons had to be meticulously planned with all the detail of an army general waging a war. Every lesson needed to be designed in a way that wasn't previously required.

For starters, each lesson must have three different learning outcomes for the pupils, basically a written expression of what you wanted your class to come away from the lesson with. Secondly, every minute in a lesson must be accounted for. What activities are you going to do? How will you set these up? What will the pupils be doing? Thirdly, each lesson needed to have a plenary. In layman's terms, a plenary is a small exercise at the end of a lesson that checks for the learning of each individual child. And on top of all this, we were introduced to the befuddling world of differentiation.

Differentiation is about making sure that the needs of all pupils are accounted for, both academically and otherwise. It's about showing how you tailored your lesson to the specific needs of a particular child. For example, it's not uncommon for one or two children in a class to have dyslexia, a condition that often needs different coloured overlays in order to read (something we happen to do quite a lot of in English.) One child might need a green overlay, another a red one. So you as a teacher need to therefore make sure that your lesson powerpoints, any worksheets or handouts, are available in their preferred colour. It's a ball ache, there's no denying it, but I always used to think it's probably far more of a ball ache from the kid's point of view. Imagine not being able to read or understand most things unless they've been passed through the equivalent of a literary snapchat filter.

In a wider context, differentiation is about recognising that within a class of 30 children there's some who'll get things more quickly than others. How do you challenge the children at the top of the class, while still making things accessible for those at the lower end? Make your lesson too easy, and the more academically capable will fly through it in no time and spend most of the hour disrupting your class, make it too difficult and the kids that find the work too tough will down their tools and misbehave in their own way. It's a balancing act that even the most seasoned educators can get wrong.

On top of all this, we had to make powerpoints for every single lesson and produce our own worksheets and any other learning aids we thought we were going to need. Lesson plans and a copy of the powerpoint slides needed to be handed to our mentors at least 24 hours in advance to be checked. Sometimes we'd get the all clear, most of the time we'd have to make changes here and there, and occasionally we'd be told to start the whole thing over again. Given that every lesson was now taking roughly two hours to plan, plus potentially another one or two hours to implement changes suggested by our mentors, myself, Saima and Andrea were all gradually beginning to fall behind.

We were being scrutinized more than ever before. The Assistant Head Of Department, Justin, was a particularly difficult man to please when he was observing your lessons. The only male teacher in the department, he'd amassed a decade's worth of teaching experience despite being just a few years older than I was. One time, he pulled me up for using the word "if" rather than "when" on a learning objective. Another time, he schooled me for not having the correct body position when examining a pupil's work. He was a relentless perfectionist and fastidious to a fault - the kind of person that has 'Days Of The Week' boxer shorts. But he wasn't doing it to be cruel or condescending, he genuinely wanted us to be the best we could be. Having said that, it came as little comfort when you'd just spent last night staying late for three hours planning his lesson to try and impress him only for him to pull you up on the size of the font you used on your sixth slide. (Yes, he really did.)

At times it felt like I was getting more wrong than right. Saima shared the same concerns, and began working later and later to rectify the issue. We began to lean on our mentors more and more for assistance. Holly was kind enough to take time out of her day to provide me with more one-to-one support, which always seemed to start off well and degenerate into salacious gossip. Her lesbian affair with the P.E teacher was still a thing, in fact far from being the cheeky fling she'd originally anticipated, she'd seen her own sexuality in a whole new light and had split up with her fiance during the October half term. Her fiance, in turn, had reacted by unequivocally supporting her new-found sexual awakening, whilst simultaneously refusing to categorise it as anything other than a superficial romp. He had told Holly that she could do whatever she wanted and, when she felt the time was right, he would be ready to take her back.

Andrea, of course, was oblivious to any and all criticism that came her way. Her mentor had worked out, not long from that fateful first meeting, that she was unable to receive negative feedback without having a near meltdown. Her Gemma Collins-esque temperament had worn thin to the point where her mentor just stopped giving her negative feedback. If she wanted to prance around the classroom calling herself "the GC" then good luck to her. For her part, Andrea took the lack of negative feedback to mean that she was amazing. In reality, it was just easier to let her think that and not have to deal with her ego.

By the time December rolled around we were all running on empty. It sounds strange, but even something as trivial as daylight hours becoming shorter were starting to affect us. There's a weird psychological impact from coming to work in the dark and leaving in the dark every day for weeks on end. The cold, wet weather starts to bite down on your morale, slowly dampening your enthusiasm. And let's not forget, schools are a breeding ground for germs. As a trainee teacher you can and will pick up every bug, every sniffle, every flu-like symptom going. It's not as though you can call in sick either, teachers are expected to work through these ailments as it's too much trouble for the school to replace you. Even if you are too ill to come to school because you're practically at death's door, you still have to send in your lessons, powerpoint presentations, worksheets and lesson plans to whoever's covering your class.

One day I was teaching a Year 8 class and checking the work of a kid named Christopher. Just as I'm reading what he's written he leant over and coughed directly in my mouth, so much so I swear as the hot air hit the back of my throat I could taste the tuna sandwich he had for lunch.

"Sorry" he sniffed, his little face totally bunged up with a nasty cold, "I've not been feeling well but Mum said I had to come into school because there's nobody at home to look after me." Three days later

I woke up with a snotty nose and a cough all of my own. Thanks Christopher, you shouldn't have.

We were three weeks away until we broke up for Christmas, but it felt like a lifetime. By this point all three of us were going round Moorfields with bags under our eyes that were so big Aldi would charge you a quid to put your shopping in them. Gradually as we became more fatigued, mistakes started creeping into our work. Andrea turned up to a lesson once with absolutely nothing prepared - no slides, no worksheet, nothing. She'd naturally assumed she'd planned for everything, but on clicking the opening slide one of her pupils put his hand up and said "We did this last week!" He was right. What followed was a short conferring between her and the teacher observing the lesson, who then had to take over from her and improvise an hour's learning on the spot.

Saima and I were slipping too. In the lesson we co-taught together, a bottom set Year 7 class, we'd been spending the last few weeks teaching them about the Dickens novel, Great Expectations. Because what better way to engage children who have a hard time writing in complete sentences than by making them read Victorian literature. I'd always thought it was ironic we were teaching this particular novel, given that they were bottom set, great expectations is the one thing none of us had about any of them. These poor kids didn't have a bloody clue what was going on - one of them even referred to Magwitch as McDonalds in his end of term assessment. I don't know what impressed me more; the fact that he'd inadvertently created his own contemporary interpretation of a 200 year old story, or the fact that he spelled McDonalds correctly. I gave him extra marks for post-modernism.

In the final week leading up to Christmas, with the end of term exam out of the way, marked, and roundly chastised, Saima and I decided to show the Great Expectations film to our class. The reasons for this were varied, partly as a treat for the kids, partly to help them visualise characters and settings, but mostly because putting on a film required absolutely no planning or preparation whatsoever and resulted in no extra marking. Grab a DVD, pop it in a computer, press play, and Bob's your uncle.

Except, when we put the DVD player in the computer, nothing happened. We tried again, still nothing. Saima sped off to the IT department while I tried to keep the class busy. When you think of a school's "IT Department", don't envisage the headquarters of Google. It's usually one or two of the most antisocial nerds in the country surrounded by old laptops and iPads, like some sort of magpie that only collects sparkly technology from 2010. Some IT support people in schools are wonderful, funny, charming and warm. So I'm told. So far every one I've met has been colder than a Yorkshire toilet seat.

I, meanwhile, try to entertain the troops whilst Saima drags one of the technology goblins from their lair in a broom closet somewhere. "Who can give me the best word to describe Pip?" I say to the class.

"Sad!" One boy shouts.

"Mad!" Says another.

A third puts his hand up. "Bad?" He asks. I'm sensing a pattern.

Saima comes back with no IT staff in tow. I begin to panic somewhat, we're way too new to improvise a whole lesson, but Saima has had an idea. "I'll bet there's a version on YouTube" she says, "you keep them busy while I find one."

Whilst I bounce around the classroom asking for different works for things, Saima does indeed find a version of the film to watch online. We load it up, press play, and breathe a huge sigh of relief. The film begins slightly differently than usual however; instead of being in a graveyard
this appears to be set by a lake. Then without warning a terrifying figure emerges from the water holding a six inch serrated blade and

shouts "Make a noise and I'll gut you like a fucking fish!"

Cue a hasty unplugging of the computer, a lesson reading in silence, and a dozen phone calls home to parents explaining that their 11 year old son or daughter was accidentally shown an 18 rated film. Perhaps most surprisingly of all, one phone call I made to a child's dad ended with him saying "don't worry about it mate, I've caught him watching porn on his phone *loads* of times." It's not that kind of 18 rated film, Mr Bennett. To this day I wonder what he thinks they teach at that school.

As Christmas drew nearer and my time at Moorfields came to a close, I thought about how well I'd settled in. The school was fantastic, the staff couldn't do enough to make you feel welcome and right from the start I was made to feel like part of the team. I was highly thought of at Moorfields; there were no doubt several members of faculty who'd cast aspersions on whether or not a comedian could make it in a classroom, but they were willing to let me prove myself.

Moorfields is a school that asks you to put a lot in, but they support you every step of the way. It's worth going the extra mile for a school like that.

As I said my goodbyes to my mentor Holly, she surprised me with a small graduation present. It was a silver USB memory stick containing every single teaching resource she had - every worksheet, every activity, every powerpoint, thousands of hours of work easily categorised into different files and folders. I couldn't thank her enough. It was a treasure trove of material that I never knew when I might need. Saima's personal mentor had done the same, and since we were in the same subject, we promptly copied the resources from each other's mentors and doubled our teaching materials. Andrea's mentor gave her a handshake, and by all accounts she was lucky to get even that.

On the final day of term before Christmas, Margaret invited us out for after work drinks. Normally I'd sooner run a mile in the opposite direction than socialise with work colleagues. It doesn't interest me in the slightest. I mean, I've just spent 40-odd hours during the week with these pricks, I don't want them eating into my weekend as well. But at Moorfields, things were different. I genuinely liked and respected all the teachers there. To get to know them as people, even for just a few hours, felt like a privilege. In fact, I'd bonded with some staff more in the last eight weeks than in other jobs I'd done for years. Perhaps the intensity of the job had fostered a camaraderie between us all.

I couldn't help but feel reluctant to leave Moorfields behind. It seemed like just when I was beginning to hit the ground running I'd been swept up and moved somewhere else. I walked out of Moorfields for the final time with my head held high and the small silver USB clutched tightly in my hand. For the first time since the course began, I felt like I at least had a safety net.

CHAPTER 7

"We try to make sure there's a variety in your placement schools" said Paul on the first day back after the Christmas half term. The ground outside was covered in a thin white carpet of ice and as we sat in the fabled port-a-cabin listening to Paul hammer on like an army drill sergeant. I swear I could see my own breath in front of me - and even that was desperate to fuck right out the door and leave in search of somewhere with central heating.

Just like on our first day in September, Paul prowled round the room, this time asking us all what we'd learned from our previous placement. Each of us took our turn to deliver one generic answer after another. "I learned to have a bit more faith in myself." "I learned to plan for the unexpected." I was tempted to tell him I'd learned my mentor was in a lesbain affair with one of the P.E teachers, but instead I made up some bullshit about being more organised.

Once again we were each handed plastic folders with the details of our second placement inside, and I nearly ripped mine open in excitement. The first placement had gone so well that I was keen to hit the ground running and make an even better success of my next school. Dumping the contents of the folder onto the table, I found the name of my second placement - St Matthews High School.

It was a similar size to Moorfields, but whereas Moorfields had an OFSTED rating of "Good", St Matthews was "Outstanding". In fact, based on their GCSE grades alone, they were one of the best schools in the county. And perhaps most curiously of all, they were a fiercely religious Christian school. Once we all had a few moments to absorb the contents of our folders, we immediately began quizzing each other to find out which of our other coursemates had got the same placement.

This time I would be placed with trainee Maths teacher and world class brown noser Anna. Hardly my first choice, but there's no way she'd be as bad as Andrea. Besides, Anna came across as a pleasant enough person in general, she was always polite and courteous, even if she did look like she'd suck the farts out of a headteacher's arse. Better to pair up with her than some obnoxious blowhard whose inability to handle even the slightest form of criticism made her a ticking time bomb so lethal I'm surprised Tony Blair didn't try to invade her on the basis of being a living weapon of mass destruction.

Just then I heard Andrea's shrill voice from across the room - "Who else is at St Matthews next?"

We began at St Matthews the very next day. I tried to arrive early to make a good impression.

Anna was already there. Of course she was. I wouldn't be surprised if she headed to St Matthews late last night, cleaned the whole place from top to bottom, baked fresh pastries for the staff room and did the school's tax returns. Andrea arrived shortly after myself and, far from being the outspoken dragon I'd come to know and dislike, she was on her very best behaviour. Credit to her, she understood this immediately for what it was - the chance of a new start.

Quickly it dawned upon us that we'd be proving ourselves all over again to a completely new set of people in a new department. We'd have to get used to new procedures, a new way of doing things, and the culture at the school would likely have a different feel to it. In many ways it was like starting again. For some, such as Andrea, this was an opportunity she grabbed with both hands. Having made such a cock-up at Moorfields, it must have been a relief to leave the place behind and move somewhere that nobody, aside from myself, knew her true colours.

For others, such as myself, it represented a needless obstacle to be overcome. I'd already proven myself once, having to do it again just felt like bureaucratic red tape. I kind of wished there was a way one school could call the other and ask if I was sound, sort of like how in prison if someone knows you then you're spared the initial hazing and accepted straight away into the gang.

We were shown around the school by our new course mentor, a dumpy woman with a bob of hair called Linda. She had a kindly face and a smile so broad and welcoming it could disarm you in an instant. Linda had run schools direct courses at the school for many years and was also, as it turns out, an Religious Education teacher.

Now normally, the R.E teacher (or Religious Studies depending on what part of the country you're in - it's very much the dinner/tea divide of the educational world) at the school isn't bestowed with any particular power. Indeed, it's not really taken seriously as a subject. Schools would like to pretend there isn't any in-build biases towards the importance of some subjects over others, but there most definitely is. English, Maths and Science are always the most important departments. They are, after all, the most coveted GCSEs. Then there's the second tier - made up of subjects like History and Languages and Geography. Then there's R.E. A subject that nobody really gives a shit about. Then finally P.E and

Music. Cue frantic complaint letters from P.E teachers up and down the country, pointing out that fields are classrooms too. I'm just joking - P.E teachers can't write.

It became searingly obvious that there was an enormous, chasm-like difference between Linda and my previous course leader, Margaret. Whereas Margaret was analytic and precise in her approach, Linda's focus was altogether more pastoral. She was more concerned with how you were feeling *deep down inside*, and facts and figures and timelines came secondary to that. I could already see I'd have some adjusting to do.

Once more we met our new mentors. Andrea's came in first, a balding man called Alan dressed in an eccentric tie designed to replicate the Bayeux tapestry. He looked like he did the bookkeeping at a mental institution. Anna's mentor was also her Head Of Department, a chap in his mid-40's called Keith. It's unusual to have a Head Of Department as a mentor, usually your HOD is an unfathomably busy person, who barely has time to wipe their arse after a shit. It's also rather advantageous as the HOD yields enough power to make sure your life is as easy as you make theirs. Get on their good side and you'll have a noticeably easier ride. Anna was smart enough to realise her good fortune and, being the champion kiss-ass that she was, immediately began puckering her lips in readiness of some good old-fashioned rimming.

When I saw my mentor, I genuinely didn't know what to make of her. She was a short, plump woman in her late 20s, with thin greying wisps of brown hair mangled on the top of her head.
She had the jowls of an English Bulldog, hanging low from her chin and resting on the top of her chest. Her neck looked like a travel pillow. And yet, there was a softness in her eyes, a longing to be liked by others. I thought about Margaret, and how unassuming she was and how tigerish she became in a classroom, and I wondered whether this was going to be the same sort of thing. She introduced herself meekly, almost as though she was more scared of meeting me than I was of her - her name was Carla.

For the first week at St. Matthews we were tasked with observing lessons. Whilst sitting at the back of a class learning GCSE French all over again isn't the most riveting of starts in a new school, it gives you an opportunity to get a feel for the place. And St Matthews felt very, very different.

The most immediate and striking difference was that lessons were between 35 and 40 minutes long, instead of the traditional one hour length standard across most schools in the country. Here there were 8 periods - two of which were 40 minutes long and the rest 35 for some absolutely inexplicable reason that nobody in the school seemed to be aware of. "It's just the way we do things here," Linda would say, as though she were in some sort of cult programmed to believe that questioning outsiders should not be trusted.

"I know," I said, pressing for an answer, "but why? Why 35 and 40 minutes *specifically*?"

"It's just the St Matthews way." She replied, eyes glazing over like her brainwashing had overridden any sensibility left in her.

The effect on lessons being so short was profound. The days felt like a sort of educational tapas, where one would barely have had a nibble of Geography and before you know it there's a big steaming plate of Science on its way. As a teacher you had to move at lightning speed if you wanted to get anything done - normally the first ten minutes of a class is spent unpacking your books, getting pens out, taking the register, waiting for latecomers, you take ten minutes doing that at St Matthews and you've already lost 30% of your lesson.

Another vast difference was the school-wide policy on silent starters. This meant that in every single lesson there was a requirement that pupils enter the room silently, sit at their desks, and there will be something on the board ready for them to engage with. It might require them to get their books out and write something, it might require them to just sit there and think, it could even be instructions to get a book out and start reading a passage relevant to the lesson. The only requirements were that there was no talking, and they were to continue with the silence until you were ready to address them.

And it worked, fucking perfectly. Even with the older pupils. They'd be in the corridor chatting with friends and showing off to one another and then, as if by magic, they'd enter your classroom and suddenly a switch would go off in their brains. It was like a mute button on a remote control. It worked like magic, but then that's the power of conditioning students eight times a day for five years.

Not all of St Matthews' school-wide policies were this useful. In fact, it goes without saying that apart from the silent starters the rest of the rules at St Matthews ranged from mildly annoying to bat-shit mental. For example, it was school policy that every lesson must have a Christian Value attached to the lesson. The "Christian Values" were nothing more than a list of things that apparently

Christians aspired to. Things like love, caring, sharing, family, strength, unity, basically any vaguely positive word was a Christian Value. And here was me, an atheist, thinking that "love" was more of a universal value, but nope, turns out that's a uniquely Christian thing. Funny how holy wars, crusades, slavery, forced conversions and torture didn't make the list.

The Christian Value had to be announced at the start of each lesson, and my goodness did they take it seriously. In one of my first lessons being observed, I remember being pulled up after the lesson for using the Christian Value "Hope", when it perhaps should have been "Discipline". I thought they were taking the piss, so I started laughing. That did not go down well and the following week Linda sent an email to us all reminding us of the importance of instilling "Christian Values".

There were other changes to get used to. At Moorfields, there was a dedicated photocopying room run by a charming woman called Mrs. Peckhurst. I didn't think it was possible for a grown person to love photocopying until I met her. Whether it was the exhilaration of printing thousands of sheets of paper every day, or the hallucinogenic properties of a dozen photocopier fumes in a poorly ventilated room, she seemed genuinely buzzed to be there. You could walk in whenever you wanted, ask for literally anything you could think of, and she'd whip it up and all the while seem extremely pleased at you for thinking of her as being up to the task.

At St Matthews, the photocopying room was run by an ex-member of the SAS. At least, that's what I assumed, given that she was never there, frequently vanished into thin air, and tracking her down seemed nigh on impossible. When there was nobody in the photocopying room, for some incomprehensible reason it remained locked so that nobody could access it. I mean, what did they think was going to happen? That I was going to sneak in and photocopy "your Christian Values are stupid bollocks" a thousand times? I absolutely would have, but that's besides the point.

During the course of the week I began to realise that St Matthews was different to Moorfields in almost every regard. Even the layout of the chairs in the classrooms was different. Moorfields favoured collaborative learning, group activities and discussion, so every table was set out in clusters across the classroom. However at St Matthews they did things the old fashioned way - rows of pupils all facing straight towards the board. Group activities were discouraged, there simply wasn't the time.

Then there were the assemblies. If you can cast your mind back to when you were a child, school assemblies were sort of like a weekly 15 minute bollocking for you and the hundred other kids in your year group. You'd come in as bleary eyed, half asleep zombies and a Head of Year would scream at you because someone's been smearing poo on the walls of the toilet cubicles and it's letting the school down. Then there'd be a quick reminder about exams that were coming up, GCSEs are important, something brief about sports teams, and if you were particularly unlucky some pre-pubescent Pavarotti would sing Amazing Grace at a pitch so high it would give migraines to all the dogs in a two mile radius.

Assemblies at St Matthews were an altogether different affair. The first time I witnessed one, I honestly thought they might end up sacrificing a kid. Maybe that's how they keep the school exams so good, every few weeks they hold a ritual and make the Gods an offering of whichever child had forgotten his homework the most. There were church organs, altar boys, they even had some kids carry a giant flag on a stick through the centre of the hall, waving it from side to side. Hymn books were handed out to students and staff alike. Far from the unceremonious dressing down of delinquents that I'd grown accustomed to, at St Matthews teachers would deliver the teachings of Jesus and other passages from the Bible, none of which involved the smearing of poo on any walls.

When the time came to observe my mentor, I didn't know what to expect. As I sat at the back, quietly observing, one thing became immediately obvious; the kids walked all over her. She'd taken to bribing them with Quality Street chocolates, so much so that she couldn't get them to do anything whatsoever without sacrificing at least one or two sweets. Even something basic like answering a question was met with "How many chocolates will I get, Miss?" Christ knows how much she spent on them every week, but I can tell you this much, last year I did the factory tour at Cadbury World and even they didn't give out as many free samples as she did.

As much as I didn't feel in a position to critique teachers, especially when I was just a couple of months into the job myself, it was obvious that Carla had a huge flaw in her pedagogy. She *needed* the children to like her. She couldn't bear the idea that any of her pupils thought badly of her, and because of this she was incapable of disciplining them. Therefore, a need for bribery had arisen. In Carla's mind, the children were following the rules willingly, and were being rewarded with sweets. In the minds of the pupils, they were following the rules for the sweets, and quite frankly couldn't give two fucks about Carla.

I watched along horrified, but I knew better than to open my mouth. I'd seen what happened to Andrea at Moorfields and didn't want the same thing happening to me at St Matthews, so regardless of how strongly I felt about the situation I kept quiet and nodded my head enthusiastically as though I were in the presence of the greatest teacher in the world. In the back of my mind I began to wonder whether or not the children would also expect sweets and chocolate from me - I didn't want them following me around the school like I was some sort of perverted Willy Wonka.

Even though I was actively trying not to, I kept comparing the routine at St Matthews to what I'd come from at Moorfields. Comparing one school with another is just about the worst thing you can do to fit in as a new teacher, it just makes the adjustment process harder. I knew this coming into St Matthews, and yet I did it anyway. The teaching wasn't as good, the school system wasn't as good, the facilities weren't as good - the only thing that was better was the exam results, and for the life of me I couldn't figure out why.

So I asked Paul. The answer he gave made me so angry I felt the hairs on the back of my neck stand up. "It's simple, really. They use the religious status of the school to decide who to take."

"What do you mean?" I asked.

Paul continued. "Ordinarily at most schools, the pupils you get are whatever turns up at the door in Year 7. You get what you're given and you have to work with that. But some schools, like St Matthews, use the fact that they're a religious school as a way of turning down kids that might be trouble. If you're a child with behavioural issues, or special educational needs, or maybe just a low academic achiever, they'll ask for proof they're regulars at a church, have attended masses regularly, take part in church life, that sort of thing. When the parents can't provide the evidence, they reject their application. But if it's a smart kid, one they know will do well, they're not bothered. As long as they know what a church looks like, they're in."

"Holy shit, is that legal?"

"How are you going to prove it? They'll say they're making checks that the children at the school share the same Christian ethos, which they're well within their right to do. And those kids they don't want, guess where they go? To the other schools in the area, like

Moorfields, who can't reject them on religious grounds. St Matthews takes all the high achievers, gets the best results, and in turn all the brightest kids want to go there so they always have their pick of the litter."

"But aren't they meant to be a Christian school? It's not very Christian to turn your back on the weakest and most challenging children and cast them off to everyone else, is it?"

"Exactly," replied Paul, "remember, the best school isn't the one with the best results. It's the one that does the most with what comes through the door."

Eventually, government policy has caught up to reflect this. In the past, schools were judged based on what percentage of their pupils got five A* to C grades at GCSE. Obviously, a large part of that depends on the pupils that come through the door. If you get an academically gifted year group, or you're from a certain catchment area where education is more highly valued, it's naturally going to be easier for you to attain those results. This government policy unwittingly penalised schools in more deprived areas where the students might not be as academically capable by using the yardstick of best exam results equals best school.

However, in 2016 the government did away with this and instead started to judge schools based on something called Progress 8. Rather than judging based on the % of A* to C grades, now schools were judged based on how much progress children made at the school. Each primary school was asked to predict the GCSE results of their Year 6 pupils and then these were measured against the results the students actually achieved. So in theory, taking a child that was predicted an A and getting them an A* was worth one point, but taking a child predicted an F and getting them a D was worth two.

The idea was to level the playing field, and it did to some extent, but as this is still a relatively new system there's a lot of kinks needing to be ironed out. For a start, you can have a bright, gifted pupil who goes through something horrendous in their personal life leading to a slip in grades that ultimately the school is held accountable for. In one school I worked at, a Year 11 pupil found her Dad dead having committed suicide during the Easter holidays. The tragic event broke her completely and she stopped coming into school. Although she'd been predicted A and B grades in most subjects, she only left school with one GCSE in Art, and even that was because it was mainly coursework based. As a result, through no fault of their own, the school received dozens of minus points as her progress technically went backwards. In reality there was nothing they could do. Of course, the real victim in this is the young lady whose future was ripped away from her, but it's a real life example that highlights the imperfections in the system.

Another far more nefarious practice in the early years of Progress 8 was 'fluffing' - a term for when primary schools would knowingly predict over-inflated grades for their pupils to make themselves look better. In the beginning of Progress 8, there was no accountability for primary schools - they were trusted to make a sincere judgement about what they felt their pupils could achieve at GCSE (don't even get me started on this, by the way. Primary teachers have no experience teaching a GCSE curriculum, so how on earth can they accurately predict how their 11 year old child will react to it?) Primary schools realised they could predict with impunity, and the better the results they predicted, the better it made them look as a school. They could stick big banners up outside their school - "90% of our pupils are predicted an A!"- and parents driving past would think "Ooooh, that must be a wonderful school, I'll send my child there!"

So, for the first couple of years of Progress 8, primary schools got away with fucking murder and there was nothing anyone could do about it. I taught children who couldn't spell words past four letters coming into Year 7 that were predicted a Grade 6 (the equivalent of a B). Now I know from five minutes of teaching them that the only chance that pupil had of getting their hands on a B would be mugging a beekeeper, but once the primary school had predicted their grades there was nothing more that could be done to change them to something a little more realistic. Then, of course, we would be tasked with the agony of speaking to parents and explaining that Mummy's Little Genius isn't sticking felt-tip pens up his nose because he's a future brain surgeon exploring the cavities of his skull, rather because he's just a bit of a moron.

There's something quite demotivating about knowing that no matter what rules are brought in to level the playing field, there will always be those that manipulate the system to their own advantage. I resented St Matthews for that, and that made it even harder for me to fit in.

After a couple of weeks of observation, we finally got the chance to start teaching lessons again. I knew this was where I could really stand out, so I was eager to showcase the repertoire of skills that had made me a Moorfields darling. To prepare for the occasion, Andrea,

Anna and I had each been given our own laptops which were quite possibly the slowest computers in existence. Mine in particular ran so lethargically when it came to measuring its speed I didn't need an IT specialist so much as a North Pole scientist that analysed the movement of glaciers.

It was painful. On top of the general frustration of watching a laptop make noises like it was about to take off into flight every time you opened an email, the laptops basically doubled the time it took to do anything. When I asked the IT team for a replacement, they told me there was nothing they could do. When I suggested bringing in my own laptop, they said I wouldn't be allowed to as it could be a safeguarding or data protection issue. I would just have to find a way to make it work.

Over time I did exactly that. My life began to revolve around making the laptop work for as long as possible. For example, each morning on the way to school I would park up ten minutes away from the school, switch the laptop on, then drive the remaining ten minutes to St Matthews. Once parked, I would take the laptop out of my car, and carry it to the staff room without shutting the lid, dexterously moving my fingers across the mouse pad every few minutes to prevent it from locking.

In my first lesson, I'd planned 35 minutes packed with activities, ideas, and one or two little

flourishes I imagined nobody at St Matthews had seen before. In my mind the lesson was going to go so well there was a genuine chance they'd think I was the second coming of Jesus and all start worshipping me. Teachers from all over the school coming to shake my hand whilst secretly checking for stigmata.

No such luck. I got to the classroom bang on time, plugged in my laptop, and started taking the register. Doing the register for the first time with a new class is always a slightly daunting experience, for no other reason than the plethora of fucking ridiculous names parents give their kids nowadays. As a teacher, you really don't want to pronounce any of these names incorrectly. It makes you look a bit amateurish, you can see the kids looking at you as if to say "Oh, you must be new, you've never taught someone called Eirian before." One time I had a girl in my
class whose first name was Abcde. I immediately emailed Reception to ask why a child's first

name had been left off the register and whether this was an administrative error, you know, rather than actually assuming that this could actually be someone's real fucking name. Turns out it was, and is apparently pronounced "Absidee". I had to break it to you, but that's not a name. That's leftover letter tiles in a game of Scrabble.

Half way through the register and my laptop cuts out completely, leaving me stranded. Instinctively I began to take a paper register so that it could be sent down to the main office and logged by someone manually. At every school, taking the register at the beginning of the lesson is one of the most important, fundamental things to remember to do. This is probably because if a kid suddenly decides to sneak off and there's a serious incident, the school could be liable.

I complete the paper register and glance over to my computer, hoping that by some technological miracle my computer has transformed from Captain Tom to Usain Bolt. Unfortunately, my computer had taken this very opportunity to switch itself off and perform an update, and I was currently on 1%. Trying to keep calm, I write a date and title on the board which I ask the class to copy into their books, hoping this will buy me enough time to figure out what the fuck to do next.

I go over to Carla to explain the situation. She offers me her own laptop if I need it, but since my lesson is only stored on my laptop, it's of no use. The pupils have copied the date and the title and are now looking at me for what to do next. I glance back at my own screen, Still 1%.

Years of ad-libbing jokes in pubs and clubs across the country had taught me how to think on my feet, and I was quite good at making it look like everything was going to plan. In the end I cobbled together an exercise where the pupils had to write a letter from one character to another from the book the class was currently mid-way through reading. I'm sure the pupils had no idea. But Carla knew exactly what was going on, and at the end of the day, she was the only one I really wanted to impress. The one good thing about teaching those ridiculous 35 minute lessons was that there's less time to fill when everything goes tits up. Afterwards we met to discuss the lesson and so she could give me feedback. Carla tried to be positive but you could tell she was wondering deep down what on earth she was going to do with me. She was looking at me the exact same way as a parent looking at their three year old's crappy crayon drawing of a house. Outwardly polite and full of praise, but inwardly trying to work out what the shit I was supposed to be. I managed to convince her that technical issues got the best of me and we should just write the lesson off as a bad job, she looked relieved as much as anything else and agreed to begin assessing me the following week. Our meeting was over half an hour long, and by the time we'd finished my laptop was on 44%.

By the time the following week came around, I walked into my next observed lesson more prepared than I'd ever been before in my life. I had a lesson on the laptop, fully loaded, ready for when the kids get in the room. I had a backup copy of the lesson on a USB drive in my pocket.

I'd also printed off back up options of the lesson on paper on the off chance both laptops wouldn't work. Hell, I was seriously considering laminating all the paper to protect it against fire and water damage.

The lesson I was teaching was centred around getting the pupils to better resonate with the character of Crooks in the Steinbeck classic Of Mice and Men. For many years, Of Mice and Men had been a GCSE text given to Year 10 classes. Personally, I think it's one of the best books ever written and, given its relatively short length and yet incredibly dense symbolism and meaning, it's almost the perfect book for students to analyse. However, when politician Michael Gove became education secretary one of his many changes was to make sure that British children were reading British books, which for some reason unbeknownst to anyone he had decided was now important. Rather than throw out hundreds of perfectly serviceable books many schools opted instead to teach Of Mice and Men earlier, usually in Year 7 or 8. Whilst it's a relief to see a classic book such as this still remain a part of a child's education, it's nonetheless an odd experience to be explaining Susy's Whore House to a bunch of 12 year olds.

For those unacquainted with the novel, Crooks is a well-educated black character who sleeps in the barn away from the other characters because he's an outcast. For my lesson I wanted to briefly touch on the injustices of the Jim Crow laws whilst relating that to Crooks as a character, showing how racial prejudices had shaped his attitudes and behaviours. A big ask for a 35 minute lesson.

When the class came in, I handed them each a worksheet and told them we were doing a simple literacy test that should take no longer than 5 minutes. The test had questions such as;

1. Draw a line around the number or letter of this sentence.

2. Draw a line under the last word in this line.

3. Cross out the longest word in this line.

4. Draw a line around the shortest word in this line.

5. Circle the first, first letter of the alphabet in this line.

6. In the space below draw three circles, one inside (engulfed by) the other.

7. Above the letter X make a small cross.

8. In the first circle below write the last letter of the first word beginning with "L".

You could see the bewilderment on their faces. One by one hands went up for help, and I told each one no further instruction could be offered. By the end of the five minutes, there were some very worried faces who thought they'd failed some potentially serious quiz.

"That was a test given to black voters in Louisiana" I said. "The tests were deliberately made as difficult as possible in order to deny black people the right to vote."

The look on their faces was priceless. As any teacher can attest, there's no greater feeling than watching the penny drop and a student suddenly "get it". In that moment, they understood Crooks better than they had before. They saw why he was wary of others, why he kept himself to himself, and why he kept a copy of the California State Civil Code of 1905 on his bedside shelf.

As I met with Carla at the end of the day for my observation feedback, I had a humongous smile plastered across my face. I knew I'd delivered a great lesson, and I felt as though I'd taken a big step to proving myself. Unfortunately, Carla didn't see it that way. She decided that a better starter would have been to use the interactive whiteboard to get the children to come and write a word on the board that described Crooks' character. I was perplexed - to me her suggestions were far worse than what I'd done, yet I knew the consequences for speaking out. The expression to "bite your tongue" had never made sense to me before, but here I was listening to Carla, and I was quite literally biting my own tongue in my mouth to stop me from saying something I'd later come to regret.

I came away from the meeting feeling confused. I thought I'd delivered a great lesson, I'd seen the lightbulb moment for the kids, and yet my feedback was relatively poor. Part of me questioned whether or not I'd let my own success at Moorfields get to my head. Perhaps I'd started to believe my own hype. Oh God, was I the St Matthews Andrea? Was it only a matter of time before I strutted round the school with an air of pomposity, carrying my dog shit laptop with the lid open and saying "actually" every other word?

The next few lessons followed a similar pattern - I'd deliver a lesson that I thought was great (and would have got me tonnes of praise at Moorfields), I'd get poor feedback, and my mentor would make suggestions that I thought were worse than what I'd come up with. By the end of the week I was second guessing myself on every decision. What once came instinctively now felt near-impossible. I felt like a football club's new signing, who'd been banging in the goals at his old club, and now couldn't seem to find the net for love nor money. Surely it was only a matter of time before my students started chanting "You're shit, and you know you are!"

On Friday evening Andrea, Anna and I had an after school meeting with our course leader Linda to see how we were settling into our new school. Anna was full of praise, of course she was. She was such a little kiss arse she could be teaching in a classroom with no roof and she'd tell the SLT how much she loved the innovative learning environment. Andrea too, seemed like she was settling in well. When Linda asked me how I was getting on, I decided that honesty was the best policy.

I told Linda I was finding it difficult adjusting from one school to another. I told her about my laptop and how many problems I was having. Finally, I told her about how I thought I was delivering great lessons but my feedback said otherwise. I spilled my guts for about five minutes straight, during which time Linda tilted her head to one side, nodded along with just about everything I said, added a few "uh-huh" and "yep" noises to show she was listening, and when I'd finished and was looking to her for some sage worthy advice, she thought for a moment and said "well, I hope things improve for you." That was it.

I'm not sure what I was expecting - maybe some advice, or offering extra support, but I came away with the distinct impression that outside of listening to your general problems, Linda wasn't one to get her hands dirty. In fact, at the end of the meeting, Linda

announced that our timetables would be increasing which meant we would be teaching more lessons. Furthermore
we would now also be responsible for marking books, and needed to acquaint ourselves with the school's marking policy. She may as well have said "Sorry to hear you're struggling, here's a shit load of extra work. Enjoy."

By the time the following week came around, my stress levels were noticeably higher than at any other point so far in the course. Finding it difficult was one thing, but I really didn't know what I could do to make it easier on myself. The USB stick Holly had gifted me, my safety net, had proven to be largely useless so far. All her lessons were timed for an hour, the 35 minute periods at St Matthews meant I couldn't draw on any of these resources. And with the added lessons and marking we were now expected to complete, it was only going to get harder.

Teaching other classes introduced me to all the other teachers in the department. Curiously for an English department, there were two teachers from America. Jenna was a young, sweet woman with a drawl of an accent that inflected at the end of each sentence as though everything she asked was a question. She was an RQT (recently qualified teacher) meaning she'd not long qualified herself and could relate better to what I was going through. Being an RQT in a school is kind of like when you see cars with those little green L plates to show the driver has just passed. It's a way of warning you that this person should technically know what they're doing but there's always a chance they'll fuck up and cause a car crash.

The other teacher in the department from across the pond was an enormous bespectacled man called Chad. He had this booming American voice that sounded like he'd eaten a megaphone. He whispered more loudly than some people spoke normally. Because of this, his behaviour management was excellent. Kids didn't talk during his lessons for the same reason you wouldn't have a conversation next to a jet engine. Chad had a frankness about him that was refreshing - he spoke his mind and genuinely seemed not to care about what anyone else thought. One time after teaching his class, I complained about a kid at the front who was making life difficult for me. "Oh Stephen?" said Chad "yeah, that kid's such a little cunt. I'd love to punch him right in the fucking face."

I don't think he even checked whether or not the door was closed.

I also had two classes a week with the Head of English, an intimidating Mancunian matriarch by the name of Susan. She looked like she'd been teaching for about three hundred years, and couldn't be more than a couple of years away from retirement. She had a reputation as a real ball buster, someone who was feared by both the pupils at the school and the staff in her department in roughly equal measure. But after just a couple of lessons teaching in front of her, I knew that I really liked her.

Like Chad in some respects, she had a candidness that I really appreciated. Schools can be bitchy places where you're constantly being judged and talked about and evaluated by others, and all too often staff were nice as pie to your face and raised their concerns about you behind your back. But Susan was cut from a different cloth. Whether it was the saltiness of her Northern working class roots, or the fact she was too busy being a Head of Department and all the work that entails, or maybe because she was so close to retirement age she could practically taste the Pimms cocktail in her back garden, she rose above the office politics. You knew where you stood with Susan. She told you when you did well, and she made damn sure you knew when you pissed her off. It frightened the life out of some people, but I'd take that approach over Linda's sit-in-a-circle-and-talk-about-your-feelings bullshit any day of the week.

I think I made an impression on Susan too. She knew that I wasn't afraid of her, and seemed to respect my honesty and earnestness in becoming a better educator. The first time she saw me teach, she waited for all the kids to leave the room and then, in that long Mancunian drawl, exclaimed "well that was actually quite good. I don't know what I was expecting, but I'm happy with that."

Feedback from other teachers had been good too, and yet I was still struggling to get positive comments from the one person who mattered most, my mentor Carla. When it came down to it, Carla was the person who'd be deciding my overall QTS grade - it didn't matter if every other teacher thought I was the best thing since whatever came before sliced bread, if she didn't think I was good enough, I wouldn't pass.

For the first few weeks, I tried almost everything with Carla. I treated her the same way I'd treat a difficult Saturday night audience that was too pissed to listen, trying different styles and approaches until something clicked. But nothing did. If I did a lesson around group activity, she'd say it wasn't structured enough. If I did something revolving more around the students working individually, she'd tell me I needed more variety or to be more engaging. Quite often she'd suggest extra things I could have done that would have, in her opinion, made the lesson "outstanding." When I reminded her that lessons were only 35 minutes long and there physically wasn't enough time to implement these changes, she'd brush this off as though it wasn't really a valid objection. Perhaps in her mind it was a reasonable expectation for me to stretch the boundaries of time itself.

And then one day, out of sheer desperation, I tried teaching a lesson as a carbon copy of her. I delivered the class as a Carla tribute act - mimicking her delivery, her pace, her tone, I even threw out a few sweets for good measure. I thought it was the worst one I'd done yet and was fully prepared for scathing feedback. She loved it. At the time this felt like a victory, but it shouldn't have.

It was evident Carla wanted to see herself in me. But every teacher has their own unique style. Some are the disciplinarians that scare the life out of the children and restore order in even the most lawless classes. Others are the empathisers, the ones students go to with their problems, insecurities and worries. Then there are the entertainers, the ones that make you fall in love with the subject. And of course there's the specialists, the teachers who know how to get the best results in the exams.

Schools are complicated eco-systems. You need a mix of all these different styles. Too many disciplinarians and the pupils will hate school and have nowhere to vent their anxieties. Too many empathisers and they'll test the boundaries and run riot. There's a delicate alchemy at place, and at the heart of it is letting every teacher develop in the style that suits them. Having an entertainer masquerade as a specialist is the same as asking an elephant to run the 110 metre hurdles. Forcing myself into Carla 2.0 felt unnatural, but I was willing to do whatever it takes to get across the finish line.

I'd been at St Matthews for about a month, when, in early February, something happened that would change the whole course of my career.

I was teaching my focus class with Carla monitoring me, when a sweet young girl called Amy innocently put her hand up and said "Sir, tell us a joke."

"What?" I asked, caught off guard by a question that seemingly came out of nowhere.

"Aren't you a comedian?"

CHAPTER 9

As soon as she said those words, I knew I was in serious trouble. This was a school where the height of rebellion and self expression was a garish tie, I didn't for one minute think they'd be overly accommodating about YouTube videos of me describing in detail what it's like to eat ass for the first time. What was curious, though, was that the rest of the class weren't shocked by these new revelations. There wasn't a flurry of hands being raised with a million and one questions, there weren't even audible gasps of shock. I quickly realised that the whole class knew I was a comedian, it's just the girl on the front row was the only one brave enough to ask me about it.

"Who told you I was a comedian?" I asked, trying to keep my cards close to my chest. I felt that in this very moment, my future on the course was in jeopardy. I didn't want to say anything now that might incriminate me further down the line.

Amy glanced to the back of the room where my mentor Carla sheepishly dug her head in her laptop, pretending to be oblivious to the drama unfolding five feet away from her. Amy turned back to face me and confirmed my worst suspicions, "Miss did."

In the heat of the moment, I made the decision to deny everything. After all, this was my focus class. If I couldn't get them to do any work because they only saw me as some sort of glorified clown, I'd fail the course and not get my QTS qualification. I needed them to believe I was worth respecting. Thinking on my feet, I dismissed Amy's question, "well, I'm sure what Miss meant
was that I'm funny in the staff room. I'm a bit of a comedian. That's probably what she meant by it."

Kids are much smarter than we often give them credit for, they can sniff out bullshit like a truffle pig in a forest. Amy's nose twitched, there was no way she bought my explanation. Rather than lingering on an explanation so thin it would make Karen Carpenter look like Andre the Giant, I swiftly moved on and began handing out worksheets and explaining the forthcoming lesson's activities. We got through the rest of the class without any further prying into my personal life, and when the bell went at the end, I bolted out the door almost as quickly as the kids. I didn't want to give Carla a chance to speak to me - I was so mad at her I knew instinctively that I was worried about what I'd say to her.

I knew straight away why Carla revealed personal information about me, I'd seen her do it several times about herself during the time I'd spent observing her. She did it as a way to connect with her pupils, purposely blurring the lines between teacher and friend in order to fulfil her need of being liked and accepted by the kids. It's in the same cringeworthy ballpark as when a teacher sits on the desk and talks in slang and gets you to call them "Mr S." or some other colloquialism.

The teacher thinks they're being 'down with the kids', but the vibe they give off is more like

someone wanting to go down on the kids. It's a creepy persona. Call me old fashioned but you're there to teach, not to make friends with people half your age.

Luckily, ever since I told Paul about my comedy back at the start of the interview process, we'd developed a procedure in case there was a leak like this. Should word ever get out about my stand up, I was to call him immediately and let him speak to the school. I went straight to my car, rang Paul, and told him what happened. When I said it was my own mentor that had leaked it to the kids, he asked me if I was sure. When I told him I was, his response was reassuring - "leave it to me, I'll sort it". There was something in his voice that calmed me down. I felt like I had the scholastic equivalent of Liam Neeson from Taken looking out for me. He had a very specific set of skills, and I was hoping making sure I didn't get kicked out of St Matthews was one of them.

The next morning I was pulled from lessons and ushered into a meeting with Paul, Linda and Carla to discuss the leaking of my personal information to the students. What followed was basically thirty minutes of my mentor trying to worm her way out of what she'd done, me getting progressively angrier with the lack of accountability from her, Paul trying to keep things professional, and Linda cocking her head to one side and nodding at everything everyone said.

"I didn't think it was a big deal," explained Carla, "I do crafts on the weekends and the kids know about that."

"How is that even remotely the same thing?!" I replied. "There's ten years worth of adult content on the internet and if the kids found that then it'll compromise me as a teacher. And anyway, if you want to tell them about your life, that's your choice. Why does that mean you get to tell them about mine?"

There was a silence in the room as Carla shifted uncomfortably in her seat. There was no explaining away what she'd done - everyone knew she'd broken an unwritten rule between teachers, never tell the kids personal information about other staff. Not so much as a first name. Because as soon as the children know about it, they will not forget it. There's a certain irony here - I must have told hundreds of children the difference between 'there, there and their' on a near-weekly basis for years on end only for them to ask the same thing again the following week completely unable to retain the information, but if you accidentally let slip something completely irrelevant information such as the Headteacher's middle name they'll remember it unconditionally for the next five years. It's almost as though their little computer-like brains store random tidbits about staff in a special folder called "Top Secret Teacher Info" that they can access at all times, but actual crucial information which will help them pass their exams goes straight into the Recycling Bin.

Linda came to Carla's rescue - "well, we can't do anything about it now. But what we can do is we can nip this in the bud. The next lesson you have with that class, I want you to go in there and admit it, and let the kids ask you as many questions as they want, get everything off their chest, then move on and be done with it. The more you play it down, the more they'll want to expose it. So let them ask whatever they want."

I exchanged worrying glances with Paul. I did not like the idea of opening myself up to the children further, in fact it went completely against my instincts of denying all knowledge. I'd spent my life actively avoiding telling people about my comedy specifically to avoid the predictable altercations that follow. It's bad enough getting questioned by adults, let alone children. Linda, however, was insistent. Paul advised me that the best thing to do moving forward was to go along with whatever the school wanted, and so reluctantly I agreed.

"However, I want to change mentors." I said.

"That's not something we usually do," responded Linda, "the problem is, it sets a dangerous precedent. What if Anna and Andrea wanted to change their mentors too? What if you changed your mentor and you were even less happy with the new one? I think it's better if we let bygones be bygones."

"But it's not about liking or disliking a person - the trust between us is broken, she stepped over a line professionally and I personally don't feel comfortable working with her now." I spoke about Carla as though she were in a separate building and not three feet away from me staring sheepishly into her bag. Linda, for her part, said she could make no promises but assured me she'd see what she could do.

A few days later I once again stood in front of my focus class and, as per Linda's instruction, I admitted everything to my class. Something about it felt strangely shameful - almost as though I was at my first AA meeting and I'd just stood up and admitted I was an alcoholic. I told the class I would answer any and all questions on the proviso that once they were finished we could draw a line under the subject and never mention it again.

Hands across the classroom shot into the air like fireworks on a cold night in November.

"Are you funny?" Yes, I am.

"Why aren't you funny when you're being a teacher?" For the same reason I don't get a room of pissed up stag and hen do's to recite Romeo and Juliet.

"Have you heard of Jason Manford?" Yes. Nice bloke.

"Can you tell us a joke?" Absolutely, but you have to wait until you're 18 and buy a ticket to one of my shows.

At the back of the room, a hand went up from a boy who'd never said more than two words to me in the two months I'd been teaching him. Usually he'd just stare out of the window quizzically, examining his surroundings with a quiet befuddlement. Sort of like a pissed bloke in a take away at 2am wondering how the hell he'd got there and where his mates were. "Sir, are you famous?" He asked.

"If I was, George, I wouldn't be here mate." The young lad seemed satisfied at the answer and, as the cogs slowly turned in his head, he realised that given a choice between chilling in a hot tub with a bottle of champagne and a gram of coke, or teaching Year 9 about adverbs, only a lunatic would pick the latter.

After about ten minutes the novelty had worn off. I once again reminded them of the agreement, that this wasn't to be brought up again and we were to draw a line under it. "I am your teacher," I repeated to them, "and that's all you'll ever know me as."
Once the lesson had ended, I headed to Linda's office. The reason for my visit was under the

pretence of letting her know I'd done what she asked and to thank her for the advice, but really I wanted to expedite the process of getting a new mentor. I had a feeling that Linda didn't take my request seriously at the initial meeting, perhaps hoping it had been said through anger. By going into her office a few days later, once she hoped everything might have calmed down, I was hoping she'd realise this wasn't an issue she could just tilt her head and nod at till it went away.

I found Linda squirrelled away in her office, buried by a mountain of files and folders. She seemed delighted that I'd taken her instruction, but when I followed up my request about changing mentors her demeanour became altogether more downcast. "I'm sorry, but I've asked around and nobody is available to take you. Everyone's just too busy at the moment" she replied.

"Well, I'll have to move schools then" I responded, hoping that she'd see I wasn't taking no for an answer.

"You'll need to speak to Paul about that. To be perfectly frank, I don't know why this has become such a big deal, it's not like you're still doing comedy."

"Of course I am." I replied.

Linda's face suddenly contorted. She went from happy mediator to sickeningly confused in an instant. "You mean, you're still doing stand up shows? Now? While you're at this school?" The concern in her voice filled the tiny room.

"Well, yeah," I said, "my bursary is only £400 a month and that won't even cover my bills, so I have to keep working."

"How have you been managing to get the work done?" Linda asked, completely mystified. It was clear she'd assumed comedy was just a part of my past, and not an active component of my life.

"I dunno, I just have."

By now, Linda's entire demeanour had changed. Gone was the smiley, head nodding pacifier, in place was a suspicious barrister cross-examining me in a courtroom. It was like Jekyll and Hyde, if one was a demure housewife in a church bake sale and the other was Tom Cruise in A Few Good Men.

Every school's culture is different. Some actively encourage a healthy work life balance, many just say they do whilst still imposing impossible expectations. But others, typically the more religious and old-fashioned establishments, seem to think that having a personal life outside of work is somehow a failing on the part of the teacher. For them there's an unwritten expectation that a teacher must dedicate their lives to the cause and act accordingly, in the same way nuns don't do 9 to 5 at the monastery and then get shit faced drunk in the evenings. In Linda's eyes, me being a teacher during the day and a comedian at night was akin to one of the nuns telling the rest of the convent she was making extra money stripping at weekends. A nun that was an ex-stripper was something she could live with, but a nun that was still dancing for dollar? Unthinkable.

At the time I wasn't overly bothered about what Linda thought of me on a personal level. I'd already realised St Matthews wasn't the school for me, but I felt like I could manage the workload and I was getting good lesson feedback from all the other teachers. Even Carla was now praising me ever since I started mimicking her. We were already in February, and I felt confident about being able to ride everything out until July.

However, looking back I now see this moment carried a huge significance. Because after this conversation, things began to get much worse. Linda had privately decided that having a comedian at the school was too big of a risk for St Matthews image. What would the parents think if they saw their son or daughter's English teacher on stage talking about fingering? Perish the thought.

Linda knew she couldn't just get rid of me without just cause. After all, Paul and I had told the school about my comedy and they didn't have a problem with it. Linda herself had actively encouraged me to talk about it with a class. But this was only because they thought I'd quit stand-up to become a teacher. They couldn't fire me because they'd made an incorrect assumption about my personal life that I'd already wilfully disclosed to them.

So instead, Linda decided that she would bully me into submission. She would raise my workload as much as she possibly could so that I physically wouldn't be able to do comedy and teaching together. If I chose teaching, she'd no longer have to worry about stand-up as my other job. If I chose stand-up, I'd have to leave the school and I wouldn't be her responsibility. Either way, she'd get what she wanted in the end.

CHAPTER 10

There are certain experiences that teachers across the country share with one another. At some point in our careers, we've all had a child swear at us. After a while in the job, it becomes a regular part of your work cycle, met with the same level of general annoyance as someone parking in your space or the people who don't wash their mugs and leave them in the sink in the break room. But the first time you see a 12 year old child screaming at you and telling you to "Go fuck yourself", it's a bit jarring. Part of you wonders where they heard that sort of language, and another part of you secretly wishes you had that level of confidence when you were their age.

Another common experience every teacher has to go through is dealing with a wasp flying into the classroom. The first time it happens you think "no big deal, it's just an insect", then roughly three seconds later the class descends into absolute pandemonium. One minute you've got thirty well behaved pupils sitting attentively ready for the lesson, the next minute it's like the scene from Ratatouille where all the rats are running around in the kitchen.

But by far the most daunting shared experience of all, the one that occupies a special space inside the mind of every teacher, is the first time you teach a sex education lesson. There's no standard practice for how sex education is taught in schools, there isn't a standardised curriculum in the same way there is for English and Maths and History. It's not like there's a test kids have to pass where they have to identify half a dozen positions, successfully operate a condom machine in a nightclub and identify the best car parks for dogging.

Every school takes their own liberties with how open and honest they wish to be about the birds and the bees. I have a friend who swears blind that in his school they gave his class different sexual positions on a worksheet which they had to identify, then they each were given a specific sexual experience that they had to explain to the class in their own words. According to him, as a 15 year old boy he had to stand in front of the class and explain what rimming was. He maintains with total sincerity that this 100% happened. Personally, I think it's a bit of tongue in cheek.

Being a Catholic school, St Matthews sex education left a lot to be desired. It was primarily focused around showing children sexually transmitted diseases in order to scare the living shit out of them. One by one I showed vaginas that looked like they'd been in car accidents and penises that looked like they'd been dipped in blue cheese and thrown in a gritter. The groans of disgust from the class got progressively louder as one by one we went through a slideshow of STDs greatest hits. Gonorrhea. Genital warts. Herpes. Chlamydia. Syphilis. Then a bunch of others even I hadn't heard of. Some of them sounded like Harry Potter spells. I was half expecting some of these kids to end up at the GUM clinic with Expecto Patronum.

After flicking through dozens of battered genitals, we moved onto the practical side of the lesson. I split the class into pairs and handed each pair a vaguely phallic bright purple pole attached to a base. I then gave each child a condom, something which in literally any other situation would have seen me arrested. I then proceeded to give a quick demonstration on how to properly put on said condom. Let me tell you this, gentlemen, it doesn't matter how many times in your life you've skinned up, you've never felt pressure like doing it in front of thirty teenagers. I felt like an air stewardess giving a demonstration on the world's perviest airline.

"Welcome to SleazyJet, tickets please."

Then it was the pupils' turn to put a johnny on what was essentially the replica dick of Tinky Winky. Condoms flew in all manner of directions as they took turns in practicing their technique. Some of them picked it up surprisingly quickly, others were terrified to even touch the thing, presumably because I'd just spent the last half an hour showing them every sexually transmitted disease under the sun and they thought even so much as touching a rubber would make their penises resemble a knackered cactus.

Before long the children had gotten bored with the condoms and plastic dicks and were finding alternative uses for them. Some kids were using them as lightsabers. One naughty lad was sticking it in the ear of the boy in front. And then, as if things couldn't get any more horrendous, a girl at the back of the class stood up with her condom and fake willy and proudly declared to the rest of the class - "Sir! I can put it on with my mouth!"

After the lesson I had a free period, which I'd already planned would be spent rubbing salt into my eyes so that I may never again gaze upon that assortment of diseased genitalia. I checked my inbox and saw I had an email from Linda. It started out fairly casually and then, without so much as a reason why, requested all of my lesson plans for the next two weeks. My jaw hit the floor so hard I bet someone in Australia felt the ground underneath them vibrate.

I didn't have the next two weeks of lessons planned. None of us did. With the 35 minute lesson structure at St Matthews, core subjects like English and Maths saw classes almost every day. It simply wasn't feasible to plan two weeks in advance because by that time we'd have had ten lessons, and no teacher knows the exact lesson they'll be teaching in ten lessons time. You have a scheme of work that you follow, a rough roadmap of how to cover everything before an end-of-term exam, but part of being a teacher (indeed a key standard by which they are judged) is their ability to ascertan gaps in learning and modify your teaching practice accordingly. If you're teaching poetry and you realise your class can't pick out poetic techniques and language devices, you don't plough on with Carol Ann Duffy and just hope the kids will pick it up along the way.

I knew I had lessons covered until the end of the week - but that was only two days worth. The remaining eight days consisted of 38 lessons. Given that it was, on average, taking me 45 minutes to an hour to plan each lesson, that meant providing Linda with what she asked for was going to take me roughly twenty eight and a half hours. I bought myself a bit of time by emailing her back with the lessons for the next two days, telling her the rest were on a hard drive at home. But even so, I was in the truest sense in the word, absolutely fucked. After school had ended, I drove straight home and worked through the night to get it done. I worked non-stop till about 2am before I was too exhausted to do any more. I took a break and worked out I still needed 14 more lessons. The only thing I could do was to take a chance and plan some group activities and maybe use some lessons from the USB stick Holly gave me and just hope that Linda didn't notice. It was a gamble, but I felt like there was no choice. By the time I'd finished fleshing out the last of the lesson plans the time was 5.30am. There didn't seem like much point going to sleep for an hour and a half, so I had a shower, got changed, and made breakfast. I'd just pulled my first all-nighter.

Still with some time to kill, I FaceTimed a comedy friend of mine who was over doing the Melbourne Comedy Festival in Australia. He was on the beach, drinking a beer and having a barbeque, and told me about the shows out there and how well they'd been going. When he asked me why I was awake so early, I made up some story about getting home late and not being able to sleep. I didn't want to tell him the truth, because compared to his life it sounded so pathetic. After we'd finished chatting I got in the car and drove back to work. For the first time, I started questioning whether or not getting into teaching had been the right decision. I guess it's only natural when your mate is on the other side of the world on an all expenses paid trip to paradise and you're working through the night for a four hundred quid a month bursary.

I arrived back at school bleary-eyed, half awake, and looking every inch like a man who'd stayed up all night. Anna and Andrea were already in the staff room, I assumed they'd also been frantically working to send Linda their lesson plans too. When Anna clocked the sight of me, her face contorted into a look of involuntary disgust, sort of like when someone shows you they're double jointed in a mysterious place.

"Good Lord, are you OK?" Exclaimed Anna.

"Yeah, I'm fine, just tired," I replied, "I had to stay up all night doing those lesson plans for Linda."

"What lesson plans?" She asked.

"Did you not get an email from her yesterday asking for all your lesson plans for the next two weeks?"

Both Anna and Andrea shook their heads. Linda's email had only gone to me. My initial reaction was to go into her office and confront her, but I was so deliriously tired by this point that I just wanted to get through the day without falling asleep mid-lesson. Storming up to her office all guns blazing, demanding why I'd been singled out, seemed like an awful lot of energy.

By the end of the day I was just about ready to collapse. I felt like a marathon runner whose legs are giving way just as the finish line approaches. Powerless to stop myself denigrating into a quivering blob of jelly. I got home and went straight to bed still fully clothed, had an hour's sleep, then set off on a two hour drive to Birmingham to perform at my gig that evening. It was 3am before I finally got home, in part owing to the two hour nap I took in my car at Sandbach service station.

By the time the following week rolled around I was beginning to feel more positive. Having to do two weeks worth of lessons in a night had nearly broken me, but now it meant that I was two weeks ahead with my work. It had been an almighty push, for sure, but now I finally had myself some breathing room. By now we were well into March, and theoretically I'd done all my planning up until the Easter holidays. Sure, those two days had been hell, but the next couple of weeks would be relatively easy with far less work to do.

Even my laptop seemed to be improving, smashing its personal best and booting up in a mere 24 minutes. Roughly the same amount of time as a full episode of The Simpsons. When I opened my inbox and saw an email from Linda scheduling a meeting for the end of the day, my confidence was so high I could only assume it would be more wonderful news. I tried to reign in the newly found spring in my step - dick-swinging is never a good look, but especially not in a catholic school. The only dicks that St Matthews were comfortable showing were the ones that looked like they'd succumbed to leprosy.

The curse of working in education is that when you're riding a wave and things are going well, you feel like nothing can stop you. Insurmountable challenges become mere bumps in the road. However, when things get tough, it can feel like the whole world is conspiring against you. Work pours in from every angle, deadlines approach seemingly out of nowhere, things that normally wouldn't even faze you now seem to dazzle you with their mere existence. Children seem to be more poorly behaved too, it's like they can smell weakness and circle you all day like jackals, waiting to pounce.

By the time the school day had finished, I was practically skipping into Linda's office. She sat me down for what she called an 'informal chat'. It took a while to realise, but schools are political organisations. Alliances must be forged, enemies will be made, double-crossing is routine. They are notoriously bitchy workplaces - every department has at least one colleague who will throw you under the bus to enhance their own career. Given that I'd been a comedian for so many years, I was totally new to this type of environment. I'd forgotten what being in a workplace was even like.

Through our 'informal chat', Linda was asking me how many gigs a week I was still doing, where I was going to and how many miles I was driving, what time I was arriving and leaving school, and unbeknownst to me, was using this information to build a case against me. For my part, I had misinterpreted the horror-stricken look across her face as admiration of my relentless endeavour of working two jobs. In reality, Linda was disgusted that I could have something else in my life that wasn't teaching. In her eyes, every night that I spent driving to Grimsby or Coventry or Carlisle was a night that I could have spent making my lessons better. To her it wasn't about me doing whatever I could to pay the bills, Linda saw it as short changing the children under my tutelage.

Later that night, Linda sent Paul an email expressing these concerns, outlining that it was "only a matter of time before his commitments elsewhere make his position within the school untenable." Paul rang me immediately to explain the situation. "Listen," he said, "it's obvious she has an issue with your *other job*. Is there any way you can knock the gigs on the head, at least until you pass the course?"

"Sure, I'd be happy to." I replied, "I mean, I'm assuming that she's also offered to pay all my bills and replace the income I'd lose?"

I took the silence down the phone as a no.

"I understand what you're saying, and I know we told them about your comedy before you came to the school and they didn't have a problem with it, but it's becoming pretty clear they didn't think you were still doing it." Said Paul, diplomatic as ever.

"Well that's their problem. Couldn't I just move schools?"

"It doesn't work like that."

"Well, where do we go from here? They want me to stop comedy, but that's not an option. Aside from the fact that I don't like them dictating what I can and can't do outside of St Matthews, I physically can't get by without the money I get from stand-up."

Paul said he understood where I was coming from but that he needed to tell me something 'off the record'. "I don't want you repeating this to anyone, but at the same time I need to give you a heads up. Linda can't kick you out just because she doesn't like what you do in your own free time. But what she can do is she can dig around until she finds proof you're doing something wrong, then she can make a case that your job as a comedian is affecting your job as a teacher."

As soon as he said that, the penny dropped. I knew right then why she asked for all my lesson plans, but not Anna's or Andrea's.

"Sounds like she's started doing that already." Paul responded. "You're going to need to keep your nose squeaky clean until July. They're going to be on you like a bad rash."

I nearly gagged. I couldn't hear the words "bad rash" without having flashbacks to that sex ed lesson.

"Oh, and word to the wise. Watch what you say. To *everyone*. Don't tell them about your gigs, where you've been, what you've done. You've no way of knowing what information will and won't get back. And by the way, there's no such thing as an informal chat."

CHAPTER 11

My first ever parents evening was spent shadowing the Head of English, Susan. As we both taught a class together, it was decided that it would be a good idea for me to accompany her in order to learn the ropes of how to successfully navigate a parent's evening. One thing you realise very quickly is this - parent's evenings are fucking pointless. The kids don't want to be there, 95% of the parents don't want to be there, and the teachers *certainly* don't want to be there. It's a well-rehearsed ballet of exquisite time wasting.

I'm sure parents evenings used to be a valuable resource, a way of creating and strengthening links between parents and teachers which can then be used to improve education out of the classroom and manage behavioural issues. Hell, I remember being *terrified* of parents' evening when I was a kid, because I knew I was a little shit and I knew my mum and dad were going to be told I was a little shit and they were going to come home and bollock me for it. I'd promise to be better behaved, and within a week I'd go right back to being class dickhead. But at least there was a consequence for my behaviour, however fleeting.

Somewhere along the way parents evenings had gone from being about holding the kids accountable to holding the teachers accountable. For decades the standard protocol was for parents to side with teachers, but in the last few years that axiom had fallen by the wayside. Now parents and their children were joining forces, combining together like shit Power Rangers to jointly complain to the teacher about how they're supposedly not doing their job.

And these are far from isolated incidents. It's become a regular occurrence. Parents would either come spoiling for a fight or simply wouldn't like what they were being told about their little darlings, so rather than accept that their child might have a problem they would instead take it out on the teacher. In their mind, their child couldn't possibly have behavioural issues - "they're always so well behaved at home, so it must be a problem with you" - oh really, do you sit them in a class for five hours a day at home and make them learn things they largely have no interest in? No? Well then. Of course they're well behaved at home, they're sitting on their Xbox all night playing games with their mates. Take that console away and tell them to do quadratic equations and see how well behaved they are then.

When I was a child, parents evenings were a behind-closed-doors affair. It was a private conversation between your parents and your teacher. But now, as with everything else about the job, things have changed. These days parents evenings take place with the pupil present in the room with you. The idea is to provide transparency, but in reality as a teacher you sort of feel like you're being ganged up on. Also, it makes it a thousand times more awkward being negative about someone to their face, even if that face is pre-pubescent and acne-ridden.

Because of this new-found tendency of parents coming to the school with axes to grind, teachers have now, out of sheer self-preservation, stopped giving out honest feedback about pupils. It just simply isn't worth being shouted at or getting into an argument. Whilst this is an understandable shift on their part, it negates the whole point of having a parents evening in the first place.

Having said that, it would be against the sacred teaching standards to flat out lie about your child. So instead teachers have developed a secret code - a way of telling you that your precious little cherub is actually a pain in the arse without you even realising. For example, if you've ever been told that your son or daughter is "very eager to participate in class", it's code for "they're always shouting out and don't know when to shut the fuck up." If a teacher tells you your child "has their own ideas which they're always willing to explore" it means they never do what they're told. My favourite idiom was when I observed Susan telling a parent that their child "liked to learn at their own pace", which was a much more polite way of saying they're a lazy sod that can barely keep their head up off the desk for more than ten minutes at a time.

Another thing of note is the huge disparity between the attitudes of the parents you meet. Some parents come to school with a vibe of "let's get this over with" - constantly checking their watch even while you're speaking to them, audible exacerbated sighs, side-on body language. I get it, they've been at work all day, but so have we. Other parents treat it with an extreme degree of seriousness; quite often they'll bring pens and paper and make notes as they're being spoken to, wanting to know every aspect of their forthcoming exams in meticulous detail. I've even had several take their phones out, put them on the desk, and record me speaking to them. In those instances it feels more like a police interview - so how is my child doing at school? No comment. What grades can they expect to achieve? No comment. I should, by all rights, have my Head of Department next to me acting like a lawyer, reading out a pre-prepared statement on my behalf so as to not perjure myself.

I applaud this level of dedication to your child's development, but these are supposed to be five minute meetings. If you're taking 15 or 20 minutes, you're taking the piss. I've been at work all day, there's 30 kids in this class, if all of them wanted a 20 minute tactical debriefing of every single aspect of the syllabus then the parents evening would be ten hours long and there'd be no teachers left because we'd all go home and we'd kill ourselves.

But by far the most frustrating types of parents are the ones that don't care enough to even show up. Because almost always, those are the parents you want to see the most. Those are the children that you're most worried about. I'm not talking about the parents that have to miss one every once in a while, that's unavoidable. I mean the ones that never answer the phone, ignore all the emails, and routinely dodge their parental responsibilities. Every single teacher cares deeply about every single one of their pupils, so much so that once a term we all willingly stay behind until 8.30pm and do a 12 hour day just to sit in a freezing cold sports hall and feed you a load of chocolate covered bullshit about your kid to keep you and them happy. Knowing that we care so much, and you care so little, that's the hardest pill of all to swallow.

Watching Susan conduct her parents evening was like watching a virtuoso at work. She deftly navigated the questions of parents, gave them everything they needed to know, and was stood up and shaking their hands before the five minutes of allotted time was even up. During the times parents wanted a more in-depth analysis of their child's performance, she encouraged them to email her directly. That way they thought they were getting a personalised service, the child kept on the straight and narrow in her classes because they thought she could just email mum or dad for the slightest indiscretion, and most crucially of all, she got to go home on time. "I've been doing this a long time," she told me in that scratchy Mancunian voice, "and I've learned this -

parents only hear what they want to hear."

It wasn't long until Paul's prediction about Linda bore yet more rancid fruit. One day, out of the blue, she sent me an email asking to see all the books for the classes I was teaching. This was bad news - theoretically she could use these to blame me for just about anything. She could scrutinise my marking, the classwork I was setting, the homework that was being done, she could even use some particularly untidy textbooks to show I wasn't meeting the teaching standard of "setting high expectations". For Linda, these books were a treasure trove of potential malfeasance.

And for good measure, rather than just picking a handful of books and hoping to stumble across something I'd done wrong, she'd chosen every single book from every class I taught. That's roughly 300 books. It's a bit like looking for traces of piss in every single swimming pool in the world. You might not find anything right away, but sooner or later it's inevitable you're going to come across it. There's no teacher alive that has three hundred perfect books. Some kids are sloppy, some have been off school and missed work, some forget their books and it slips through your marking system. As I made the second of four trips needed to put all the books on her desk, I'd already made peace with what was about to happen. She was going to find what she needed to find by hook or by crook. When I asked her why she was asking for all my books and nothing off Andrea or Anna, she muttered a barely coherent response about them not having given her any reason to believe they weren't doing what was asked of them.

The following day I was ushered into a meeting with Linda and my mentor Carla, with whom my relationship had deteriorated so badly that we barely made eye contact any more. By the look of the enormous, shit eating grin adorned across Linda's face, I knew she was about to take me to the cleaners.

Apparently I hadn't been marking according to the school's strict 'marking policy'. I told her there was a pretty good reason for this - I didn't know the school even had a marking policy.

Wasn't that the sort of thing that my mentor was supposed to make me aware of? Had my mentor not been checking my books and if not, why not? Surely, I argued, this wasn't a problem with me, it was yet another problem with her.

"Now now, you can't go blaming *all* your problems on your mentor." Linda shot back in a tone so condescending it made me want to jump over the table and strangle her harder than the final moments of David Carradine. "At the end of the day, we need consistent marking across all teachers in all subjects. It's very important. Which is why we're going to put you on a specialised action plan to address these issues. We're going to be checking your books every two weeks to make sure they meet our standards. I know usually we ask teachers to mark books every three weeks, so this might be a little…. intensive for you."

The pause in her voice was deliberate. It was her way of letting me know that she was upping my workload considerably and there wasn't a damn thing I could do about it. I did some quick mental arithmetic - it took me an average of ten minutes to mark a book and there were 300 that needed to be marked every two weeks. That works out at an extra 50 hours of marking, an extra 25 a week. Linda had just increased my working life by five hours every single day.

"Hang on, so you've said there's a problem with my marking, and even though it's not technically my fault because nobody's told me to mark like that, your solution is to increase my marking? Surely it would make more sense to decrease my marking so I can spend more time concentrating on getting it right?" The logic made absolutely no sense to me.

Linda listened to what I said with her head cocked to one side, nodding along in her usual peculiar fashion. When I'd finished making my case she simply replied "Well perhaps it's time to make some sacrifices." Sacrifices like comedy. And sleep. And eating, socialising, showering, and generally doing anything other than marking hundreds of books. But there was a determination inside of me not to let her win.

Once I had a copy of the St Matthews official marking policy, I could see that what I'd been doing wasn't vastly dissimilar to their guidelines. The main gripe was that I'd been making general comments at the end of their work about what I liked and what could be improved. What I needed to do instead was write WWW (which stands for what went well) and a positive comment, and then EBI (even better if) with something that they could do to get a better mark.

Basically the same as I'd always done, just formatted slightly differently. It seemed to me like a ridiculous thing to pull me up on, but I knew better than to poke the belly of the beast. All that would happen is Linda would search for some other infraction to drag me over the coals.

Within a day or two, the reality of just how much Linda had shifted the goalposts had fully dawned on me. It simply wasn't possible to spend five hours a day marking on top of a full day's teaching. Instead I would have to either find a way to reduce the amount of time I spent marking, or make the time up elsewhere. In the end, I opted to do both. Weekends, once reserved for spending time with my partner, were now split into two eight hour days of solid book marking.

Predictably my girlfriend wasn't exactly enamoured with the idea. She barely saw me enough as it was, and for her this was enough to question the foundations of our relationship.

It was only after one of those "serious talks" you get in relationships where I reassured her this wouldn't be permanent that she agreed to forgo what little time she had left with me for the next few weeks if it meant being the difference between passing and failing the course. It felt like going into the boardroom on The Apprentice, having to routinely state my case and why my business plan (sorry, relationship) was worth investing in. It could have gone either way but, in the end, she stuck by me.

That's something that nobody tells you about teaching. It's not just yourself that has to make sacrifices; it's everyone around you, too.

Finding time to manage my ever-expanding workload was only half the battle. I was under no illusions - doing what was asked of me was unsustainable. I was a human rainforest, and every day Linda cut down a few trees. I needed to work smarter if I was ever going to get through this. After doing a bit of research online, I discovered I was far from the first teacher to ever reach this epiphany about marking books, and there were dozens of innovative time-saving tricks and techniques to try, everything from getting pupils to mark each other's books to getting them to create their own mark scheme. One particularly ingenious teacher said he'd stopped marking work altogether, instead he would only tell his pupils how many mistakes they'd made and let them find and correct it themselves.

After a couple of weeks, Linda reviewed my marking to see if it had improved significantly enough to take me off her action plan. Out of three hundred books, she found five mistakes. This was enough to see me put on the action plan for another two weeks, despite me pointing out that it meant I had a 98.33% success rate. Apparently, that's not good enough. It felt like failing a driving test because of a twisted seatbelt, but I knew full well that kicking off about it was exactly what Linda wanted. If I gave her even a hint that the marking was getting to me, she'd keep me on it all the longer. I had to act unfazed and hope she'd lose patience and move onto finding other ways to antagonize me.

A week later and that's exactly what happened. After once again finding myself at the mercy of Linda's 'review', normally about as biased as a North Korean courtroom, she decided to take me off the marking plan just in time for Easter Holidays. Clearly she thought whatever she was doing wasn't working and had opted for a different approach. I tried to maintain an air of nonchalance, as if it didn't really matter one way or the other, but my poker face was struggling to contain my sheer relief.

Truth be told, three weeks of having my marking audited was enough to make me want to quit teaching forever. Even employing every time saving technique I could find, my marking was still adding 20 hours a week to my workload, and I was having to work two extra hours a day plus five hours a day on weekends just to keep up. Then on top of that I had lesson planning and staff meetings and detentions and all the other admin bullshit they make teachers waste their time doing. Then I had my comedy gigs on top. Never mind spending time with my partner, I hadn't done anything that wasn't school, sleeping, comedy or marking in almost a month.

CHAPTER 12

Whenever I told anyone I was training to become a teacher, they would inevitably mention something along the lines of "think of the holidays". There's a perception amongst the general population that teachers spend their half terms on exotic trips away, glugging sangria on golden beaches and having unprotected sex with the locals like a lads holiday in Magaluf. In reality, most of the time is spent preparing for the following term or, more likely, catching up on work left over from the term before. That's not to say we don't occasionally have days out, lie-ins, and nights out getting pissed in the middle of the week (you haven't lived until you've been shitfaced on a Wednesday as an adult), but it's certainly not the party infested mass orgy certain newspapers would have you believe.

In truth, teaching kind of reminded me of doing High Intensity Interval Training. Ask any Crossfit enthusiast about HIIT and they'll tell you it's a way of working out which revolves exercising at your absolute maximum, then having more time to rest and recover. It's the opposite of, say, walking on a treadmill for an hour. If you don't know any Crossfit enthusiasts, they're easy enough to find. They're the ones with arms that look like they're been made by gluing elephant testicles together and necks as non-existent as their personality. If you're still not sure, strike up a general conversation with them. If they do Crossfit you'll know within 30 seconds, because they'll have somehow managed to segue it into the conversation.

The intensity of teaching very much reminded me of this kind of work out. You'd work 60 hour weeks for a couple of months, have a week or two off, then repeat the process. The exception being, particularly in your first few years, as soon as you'd stop off the treadmill all sweaty and breathless, someone would stick half a dozen books under your nose to mark. If teaching was a work out, it would be called Sustained High Intensity Training - partly because it's relentless and just never fully stops to give you a moment's rest, but mostly because it spells SHIT for short.

Taking stock of my journey so far during the Easter break, I realised Linda's campaign of harassment had affected me more than I liked to admit. Aside from the sheer amount of extra work she'd piled on me and the fatigue with which it induced, I'd begun to see the profession in a far more cynical light. Worse still, I actively hated the school I was at. The more I tried to push it out of my mind, convince myself that it was just Linda and Carla that were the problem, the more I found a festering resentment for St Matthews.

Every single facet of the school I seemed to disagree with; the ridiculously short lessons, the nonsensical "Christian Values" we had to jam down our students throats as though they were in any way relevant, the overall snobbery and elitism of the school. Linda may not have succeeded in stopping me from doing stand up, but she'd absolutely succeeded in making me feel like I didn't fit in.

It seemed as though St Matthews and I were mutually incompatible - they wanted the prim and proper style teacher from 50 years ago, and instead they got me, a big bearded man who looks like someone's dressed a homeless person in a suit for a bet. They weren't about to change for me, and I certainly wasn't about to change for them. To highlight just how low relations between myself and the school had sunk - in one lesson just before the Easter half term, whilst being observed by Carla, I took off my blazer and taught the lesson in my shirt and tie. I didn't even think anything of it, the room was incredibly hot and I was simply making myself comfortable. Unbeknownst to me, I almost caused a national incident. As it turned out, several of my tattoos were clearly visible under the white shirt I was wearing. As far as Linda and Carla were concerned, seeing a faint outline of a tattoo was akin to me jumping on the desk, lowering my pants, and windmilling my cock in the faces of the Year 8s.

Rather than simply take the warning, I asked Linda and Carla what I was supposed to do instead? Would they rather me continue to work in 30 degree temperatures in a tweed jacket? Sweat pouring off me like Oscar Pistorius on a murder charge? Or would they prefer for me to take a scouring brush to my left arm and simply scrub off the full sleeve of tattoos I sported? Perhaps they'd like to pay for me to go shopping and buy some shirts in less opaque colours? I could be the Julia Roberts to their Richard Gere. In the end Linda gave up lecturing me. Clearly it wasn't as appealing now I was so far at the end of my tether I'd taken to fighting back.

There was no doubt in my mind, I was at my breaking point. During the Easter half term I decided enough was enough - if Linda was going to keep targeting me I was going to quit. I didn't come to this decision lightly, in fact a large part of me was disgusted with the idea of her 'winning'. But I reasoned that qualifying as a teacher was a bizarre length to take to spite someone. I'd already begun to resent the profession and I was, what, nine months in? How was I going to feel in a year or two? Was it even worth carrying on, knowing I was edging closer to the door before I'd even officially started?

I thought about my partner - was it worth putting her through much more of this? Could our relationship even survive it? But then, if I gave up now, everything I'd already put her through would all have been for nothing. Then I thought about my parents, how proud they'd been when I told them I was going to be a teacher. Giving up felt like letting them down, and I felt like it would make them lose faith in me too. No longer would they look at me and see a grown-up, an educator, with his life mapped out and firmly on track. I wanted them to feel like I'd accomplished something and not feel embarrassed when other parents asked what I did for a living.

After two weeks of soul-searching introspection, I made the decision to stick with teaching. After all, I was so close to the end of the course, it seemed silly to throw it all away. However, I also wasn't going to be taking any more of Linda's shit. I made a promise to myself that if she were to continue down the path of the last few months, I was going to throw in the towel and have no guilt about doing so. I actually fantasised about dropping everything and walking out of the school in a blaze of glory. Screaming and shouting like I was on the trading floor in Wolf Of Wall Street, snorting copious amounts of cocaine off the laminate school floor and kicking Linda square in the tits.

When I came back to St Matthews after Easter, I was spoiling for a fight. I was the short bloke in the rough pub, stood at the bar hoping someone would spill my pint or look at me the wrong way so I had an excuse to kick off. The kids could sense my mood had changed, and they did their best to avoid me at all costs. You'd be surprised how quickly reputations are forged in school - all it takes is for one pupil with a big enough mouth. For me, that pupil came in the form of a Year 10 child called Adam. He had his first detention with me and, rather than let him sit in silence doing nothing, I had him copy out a Wikipedia article about the history of air-conditioning units. When he refused, I had him back again the following day. Before I knew it, I'd become known as someone who was not to be fucked with.

One day I was walking through a building with extremely narrow corridors on the way to teach a lesson. These corridors were so small there was a one-way system in place just so people could move through the damn things. They were a tight fit for a child, but for me, an 18 stone fully grown man, I didn't so much walk through the building as I did wear it like a large jacket. It was like trying to fit a canal boat in a drainpipe. Behind me I could feel a couple of pupils trying to barge their way past me and I could hear one of them sounded like they were crying hysterically, the sort of cry where tears stream down your face and you take lots of slow little breaths to try and control yourself. Clearly they were embarrassed about crying in public and were trying to make their way past me to go somewhere quieter until they calmed down.

"No," I thought to myself, "why should you push me out of the way just because you're having a bad day?" And with that, not only did I not move for them, but I walked even slower just to be an arsehole. Sort of like when you're driving and a BMW comes right up your arse so you drive at a snail's pace just to piss them off. As I turned into my classroom, these kids darted past me like their lives depended on it. I looked round to see who had the gall to shoulder me to one side. Turned out they weren't crying at all. One of them was having an asthma attack.

I fully expected this to get back to Linda who would then reprimand me for not living up to the sacred Christian Value of not moving out the way quickly enough, or something equally incredulous. But nothing came of it. In fact, she'd not so much as emailed me in a couple of weeks. Bizarrely, it felt like the more I actively tried to attract Linda's ire, the more she seemed to leave me alone.

She'd gone from being like a wasp, constantly buzzing around me threatening to sting me at any moment, to some sort of house cat completely unmoved by my existence and unwilling to engage with me no matter how much I tried. At first, I feared the worst. I thought the reason Linda wasn't all over me like chlamydia in a Blackpool bed and breakfast was because she was busy plotting her next move in orchestrating my downfall. Clearly it was something so monumentally Machiavellian that it was taking up all her free time, and the sword of Damocles was no doubt dangling precariously above my head.

Paranoia began to set in. Had she forgotten about me? Had she lost interest? Had she been reprimanded? Did one of the other trainees piss her off even more than I'd done? I'd barely seen Anna or Andrea since before Easter, perhaps something had happened to them? Maybe Andrea had punched her mentor because he gave her a small dose of constructive criticism, or maybe Anna finally had that long overdue stress-induced nervous breakdown and was currently locking herself in one of the Maths classrooms smearing her own shit on the walls.

Incredibly, the Head Of English Susan even took me to one side and asked if I'd be interested in applying for a job as an English teacher at the school after I qualified. I told her I wasn't interested; officially the reason I gave was that I was looking for part-time work, but the real reason was that I still hadn't forgiven the school for how I'd been treated. Even though things were OK now, I still felt very much like an outsider. If the school was one big family, I was the teenage foster child. Grateful that I'd been allowed to stay, but with not so much an ounce of feeling like I actually belonged there.

Besides, I had my own interviews lined up. The first was at an inner city school in Manchester. I'd applied for the position because during my short teaching tenure I'd realised I far more enjoyed working with challenging and difficult pupils than I did with high achieving pupils. It felt like there was more of a sense of accomplishment because there were so many more barriers to overcome. There are some kids that are so academically gifted at times it feels like you could lock them in a room for ten years with nothing but textbooks and they'd come out with a doctorate. I preferred the ones that looked like they'd rip off pages of the textbooks to use for roaches.

Interviews at schools require a lot of preparation. Usually they will last for half a day or more, during which you'll be expected to teach a lesson and be interviewed by a panel usually consisting of the Headteacher, Head of Department, at least one Assistant Head, plus anyone else vaguely important that they can squeeze around the table. Some schools play with the format even further and have you interviewed by a panel of children too in order to 'see how you interact with them', which is code for seeing whether or not you can be polite enough to mention what a colossal waste of time it is.

As I arrived at the school's reception, I had a visitor's badge printed off (basically a lanyard that says "I'm not a teacher, but I'm not the world's most daring paedophile either") and was sent to the English staff room to wait for the process to start. The room was fairly small and was made to feel positively claustrophobic by the twenty or so people crammed inside. Over half were interviewees like myself and the rest were members of faculty. I was smart enough to realise they hadn't put us in this room for no reason - they wanted to see how we'd get on with their existing members of staff. Some interviewees sat quietly, browsing their phones and checking their social media, but I made a point of striking conversation with several teachers which seemed well-received.

One by one our names were called to deliver a short twenty minute lesson on analysing a piece of nonfiction. Learning the lessons from my calamitous interviews when trying to get onto the course, I came ridiculously well prepared and didn't try to cram in too much. I aced the lesson, jutting around like a veritable performative peacock. After we'd all done our lesson, the Head of

Department came in and read out about eight names and took them outside. They didn't come back. Just like that they'd been evicted, presumably Davina McCall was hanging outside the school gates waiting to interview them all about their time in the process.

As the teachers began to disperse, the four of us interviewees were left alone with one another, exchanging pleasantries and quietly sizing up the opposition. The usual questions were batted about, what school are you in, is this your first year teaching, and so on. One woman sat in the far corner of the room, sheepishly avoiding eye-contact. I tried bringing her into conversation and asked her what school she was currently working at.

"Oh," she said softly, "this one."

I tried to act calm, but immediately I sensed a set-up. Over the course of the next five minutes she'd told me she went to this school as a pupil, volunteered here after graduating from university, was encouraged to train as a teacher by senior management, was best friends with the Head of Department and was engaged to another one of the English teachers. Basically, my
chances of getting a job were about as slim as Harold Shipman getting a knighthood. The

interview itself was because the school knew it was legally obliged to advertise for the role. The dozen applicants was to make it look like an official hiring process.

In reality, there was absolutely nothing I could do or say that would get me this job. Because of this, surprisingly I had one of the best face to face interviews I've ever had. I played without pressure, and I have no doubts that had the game not already been rigged I'd have been offered a job.

At the end of the day, the remaining candidates have to wait around while one by one they are called into a separate office. They are offered a job there and then - and it's up to you to accept or decline. If you accept, the remaining candidates will be notified and you'll officially take the role. If you decline, you'll be dismissed and they'll offer it to whoever was their next choice.

This process repeats until someone accepts the job. This makes for a unique experience because from the minute you step foot in the door not only are you trying to impress the school, but they're trying to impress you. Hiring staff is a costly, time-consuming exercise, and schools are notoriously bereft of both time and money. The more times they have to interview for a role, the more of the aforementioned it consumes, so they'll offer you the job before you leave the building and once you've said yes it's a professional courtesy to honour that agreement no matter what happens. As a candidate, the process also puts you in the unenviable position of knowing whether or not you were the faculty's first choice. Quite often you're left in the staff room on your own, waiting to find out if they'll even offer you the job, feeling very much like an ugly teenager in a nightclub at 4am after all your mates have hooked up.

To the surprise of absolutely nobody, the job went to the girl who already had her foot, leg, arm, shoulder, head and most of her torso in the metaphorical door. I drove home contemplating what a gargantuan waste of time it'd been for everyone. By now we were approaching June and the pressure to find a job was very much on. Many of my course mates had already been offered roles in schools once they qualified, Anna had been given a place in January, but I'd found myself somewhat behind the curve and now was in danger of being left on the scrap heap.

This was, in part, down to my preference for part-time work, which is far more scarce, but also because Linda had taken up so much of my time making me jump through hoops that I'd barely had a chance to apply for positions. But now the situation was becoming desperate, if you don't secure a job at the end of your teacher training, it becomes even harder the following year as schools assume there's something wrong with you. They see you as the runt of the litter.

The next day at St Matthews, the Head of Department Susan asked me how the interview had gone. I relayed the full story and she barely flinched. Apparently this was a common occurrence - schools regularly have their candidates already picked out and the interviews are a tedious formality that everyone has to endure. She then remarked upon how she was struggling to recruit for the English role here, and asked me if I'd reconsider my initial rejection. Again I told her no. I wanted a fresh start. Even though my jobless future was worrying, I knew it was far worse to hastily accept a job I wasn't suited for, and even Stevie Wonder could see I wasn't a good fit for St Matthews.

In the final week before the June half term, I had another interview at a school in Wigan. I arrived just in time to see a ten man brawl at the school gates. Punches were being thrown, bags were being swung like makeshift battle axes, and the on-duty teacher was trudging up the drive with all the urgency of someone unloading a dishwasher. In the car park, I took a look at the school. The far entrance was covered in graffiti. There was litter everywhere. It looked like what would happen if they remade Grange Hill and set it on the Gaza Strip. I didn't feel comfortable even leaving my car here, so I didn't. I drove off.

The following day I was in the staff room at St Matthews, contemplating accepting their offer. Sure, I hated the school, didn't trust half the staff, and Linda had driven me to the edge of paranoia, but at least nothing was on fire. At least I knew I could get through a school day without seeing teenage Wiganers engaging in a Royal Rumble. At that moment, an assistant headteacher with whom I'd never spoken approached me. Goodness me, I thought, they're really bringing out the big guns to convince me to come here.

He stood in front of me and said six words that immediately turned my world upside down.

"The kids have found your videos."

CHAPTER 13

It took a minute for it to sink in. He was ashen faced as he was telling me, like some general on the doorstep of a housewife, delivering news that her husband's plane had crashed at sea. The gravity of the situation at the time was somewhat lost on me, indeed if anything I was surprised it had taken the children four months to find them since they found out I was a comedian. I'd always assumed that one would inevitably follow the other and that the school was prepared for that. Apparently they weren't.

"I'm going to have to pull you out of lessons today while we sort this out" he said.

The assistant head led me through a labyrinth of corridors like he was smuggling me through the school. We arrived at his office, and he led me in the room adjacent to it, which is usually reserved for naughty pupils who have to be put in isolation. I sat in the room waiting for someone to come along and explain to me what the hell was going on. I expected to be waiting ten or fifteen minutes, but when an hour had passed and nobody had come to check on me I began to fear the worst.

At first I tried to explain it away by rationalising that today was the day before the June half term and was therefore the school's Sport's Day, an anarchic day of teenagers running round a field whilst the fat asthmatic kids cheered, or rather wheezed, them on. At a guess roughly 90% of the school was involved in what is essentially The Puberty Olympics, the remaining 10% were children who opted to remain in lessons for whatever reason. Usually the quiet 'school shooter' types, and ginger students for whom being in the sun all afternoon was tantamount to a death sentence.

Even so, something felt off. The way that I'd be dealt with, shuffled through the school like I was a bag of drugs going through customs, it slowly dawned on me that perhaps this wasn't a situation that could be explained away. They didn't want anyone seeing me, hence why I was locked in the far corner of the room as if I was the St Matthews Quasimodo. A horrible thought crossed my mind - what if they kick me out of the school?

The more I thought about it, the more I realised that was exactly what they were going to do. Oh God, what about my evidence file? Would I even get to pass the course? To come this far and to be told I couldn't finish would be intolerable, it would be like running the London Marathon and then being told that there was a road closure for the final 200 yards. I had originally planned to use the June half term to get my evidence folder together, but if I got kicked out of the school I'd be booted off their systems before I'd even got home, with no way of recovering the "evidence" I'd need.

Frantically I opened my laptop and began copying every single thing I could find onto a hard drive. I didn't know what I was going to need, or even how long I had, so I figured it was better to copy everything and not need it than to be selective and miss something important. At any moment a member of staff could walk through the door and lead me to my fate, and unfortunately for me I had to work with a computer so slow it made Captain Tom look like Usain Bolt.

Another hour and a half went by and I'd finished copying everything I needed, but still nobody had come to even check up on me. I sat at my computer, wondering what to do next. After a little while, Linda entered the room. Finally, I was going to get to the bottom of what was going on. "I know you're up here on your own," Linda began sheepishly, "and I know you've finished your marking for your Year 10 assessments, so I was wondering if you wanted to use this time to mark some other classes too? Just to help your department?"

I lost it. "Are you fucking serious?! You drag me out of lessons, lock me in a room near enough three hours without telling me what's going on and you come up here and ask if I want to do OTHER PEOPLE'S MARKING?! Fuck off."

It was the first time I'd sworn directly at anyone since I got here, and now I was basically telling my boss to go and fuck herself. Linda, same as always, cocked her head to one side and nodded intently like a retarded puppy, her signature body language. At that point I knew with as much certainty as I could gather that I was going to be kicked out of the school. The way Linda just stood and smiled while I told her to fuck off, she knew it didn't matter. She'd won.

When the bell rang for lunch I was still stuck in the isolation room, still having not been told my fate. I got my lunch out of my bag then stopped as a thought crossed my mind. Why was I locked in here like this? Why should I be? I've not done anything *wrong*, all I've done is what they told me to do, so why was I being punished? As an act of defiance, I grabbed my lunch and headed to the staff room to have lunch with everyone else.

Walking into the staff room was a surreal moment, everyone was looking at me whilst at the same time trying to avert eye contact. In schools, gossip travels fast, and it's often a bastardised version of the truth. I sat down with Anna and Andrea and ate my lunch whilst being bombarded by questions from them both. In the far corner of the room I saw Carla watching me. At no point did she even attempt to come over and speak to me. I was going to be kicked out of the school at any moment because of something she had done, and yet she couldn't bring herself to even utter two words to me.

The assistant head was in there too, and as soon as we'd both finished eating he came over to me. "We're ready for you, if you'd like to follow me."

I was led into the Headteacher's office like a naughty boy, and inside I was joined by the Head and her two assistant headteachers, and also my course leader Linda. It felt like being on trial for murder and seeing the jury was made up entirely of the victim's friends and family.

The Headteacher, an intimidating woman with a gaunt face and a long nose that looked remarkably like one of the crows in Dumbo, began her inquisition. "We've had complaints about you from parents because of the content you have online."
"Right, well, I told you about this back in February and I was told by Linda that it didn't matter. So why are you telling me now, in June?"

"Can you please explain this for me?" Said the Headteacher, sliding across a piece of paper face down on her enormous wooden laminated desk.

I turned the paper over, there was an email exchange between the Headteacher and a parent, during which the parent had sent an attachment of a screenshot of an instagram post of me on stage with a giant dildo stuck to my head.

The post was from a show four years ago and posted to a private instagram account. This parent must have found me on the platform, specifically requested to follow me, then scrolled through hundreds of pictures before they found something incriminating. What a waste of time, considering they could have typed my name into YouTube and found hundreds of hours of inappropriate content straight away.

To make matters worse, I recognised the surname instantly. It was the parent of a girl I taught in Year 8, a quiet girl who often got picked on and with whom I'd been exceptionally kind to, letting her sit with friends, making sure she was with people she liked during group tasks, doing all the coaxing and nurturing I could to help her come out of her shell and gain a bit of confidence. It's a pity the parent couldn't have seen pictures of me doing all those things.

I stated my case to the head and her panel of cronies, but I knew it was no use. I told them about how my mentor had told the children I was a comedian and, had she not done this grossly inappropriate action, we wouldn't be where we are now. I told them how I made Linda aware of the content and she specifically told me to admit I was a comedian and hold an impromptu Q&A session. I made it very clear that I felt like I was being punished for doing the very things they told me to do. None of this was actually my fault. They knew I was a comedian when they took me, their staff told the kids, they told me how to react, and now, four months later I'm being kicked out because those videos I told them existed have been found to indeed exist.

The Headteacher listened intently, but she was more interested in letting me say my piece than having a discussion or changing her mind. The outcome was inevitable. When I'd had my say, she confirmed what I'd known all day. "Well, regardless of the circumstances which I'm sure are regrettable, we can't have you at the school any more. Your position as a teacher has been compromised too much."

And with that, the two assistant headteachers escorted me off the premises. You know, like a criminal. Like I'd been caught trying to steal one of their ancient laptops or fingering a Teaching Assistant.

I didn't get to say goodbye to any of the children I'd dedicated my life to for the last six months. When Andrea and Anna left, they got gifts from their departments and a signed card from all their classes. I missed out on all of that. In the space of 48 hours I'd gone from being offered a job for the second time to being forcibly ejected and erased from the school's history.

To me there was a telling irony that in a school that were so fiercely proud of their Christian values that I had to incorporate one into every single lesson, they failed to actually stand by these values when it came to me. When push came to shove, they showed absolutely no compassion, or forgiveness, or understanding, or any of the other bullshit. They preached, but they did not practise.

When I got to my car I rang Paul, who was incredulous at not being told by the school. He apologised to me profusely, stating that St Matthews hadn't followed the agreed protocol and that, were he in the meeting, he would have defended me. None of this was much good now of course, the sentence had already been passed. The death penalty had been issued and here I was, sat in the electric chair, while a lawyer tells me he would have represented me had he known about it.
"So what happens now? Do I still get to pass the course?" I feared the worst.

"I'll be honest, I don't know. This has never happened before. Let me make some calls over half term, but right now, I can't promise you anything. I'm sorry." He replied.

The gravity of the situation began to overwhelm me. I'd worked 60 hour weeks every week for almost ten months. I'd thrown everything into the course; every single ounce of my free time, I'd sacrificed my relationship, time spent with friends and family, and my stand up career had stagnated. I'd put my life on hold to do this and here I was, at the very final hurdle, having it snatched away from me for reasons beyond my control.

It was crushing. I turned the car engine, reversed out of the St Matthews car park, and as I drove home with the radio off I started to cry.

CHAPTER 14

I spent the June half term on tenterhooks, not knowing whether or not I'd be able to actually pass the course. Initially Paul had thought that I might be able to just finish the course early, having accrued enough hours inside a classroom despite my early expulsion, but upon inspection he informed me that I was just ten hours short of the minimum threshold. The focus was therefore shifted on finding me a temporary placement to "see out" the rest of the course. It felt like being an animal waiting for adoption, each day wondering whether or not I'd find a new own or end up as an ingredient in a value meal lasagne.

Lo and behold there was one school who stepped up in my time of need; Moorfields.

Graciously they offered to have me back for the final month of the course, with enough flexibility to do as little or as much teaching as I wanted. Holly resumed her role as my mentor, now back with her fiancé after her lesbian fling proved to be exactly that. When I asked her about her moment of realisation that batting for the other side was more of a loan move than a permanent switch, she replied "I woke up one morning and I was like, you know what, I actually really miss penises." Fair enough. In the past I've felt the same about Vanilla Coke.

As it happened, I ended up doing more than my fair share of teaching, on account of the fact that my all important evidence file was practically non-existent. It was so thin, even Karen Carpenter would've looked at it and thought "that's taking things a bit too far". We spent the last month working together to complete the folder of evidence so that I ranked as "outstanding" against the teaching standards.

Holly even helped me prepare for another interview I had coming up. The school in question had left it incredibly late in the day to employ someone, but for me this was very much my last chance saloon. Even though it was a full time role, I had run out of options. You see, for prospective teachers, completing your PGCE is only half the battle. Once you finish your year as a trainee you gain QTS (Qualified Teacher Status) which you can then use to apply for a job as an NQT (Newly Qualified Teacher). Once you have finished a year as an NQT, only then are you deemed a proper "teacher". If you do not complete an NQT within five years of passing your QTS, then your QTS runs out and you must start all over again.

The school in question was Fairhaven Technology College - a school in one of the roughest areas of Preston. Upon first inspection, you notice that the school has been particularly liberal in it's adoption of the moniker "technology" and "college", given that there were roughly about 50 iPads between a thousand pupils at the school and they were hardly ever used, and the "college" consisted of a dozen or so girls doing a hairdressing course. It was a bit like me calling myself a footballer because I play 7-a-side once in a while.

It's not uncommon for schools to jazz up their names a bit to appear modern and futuristic to prospective pupils, but they usually back it up with some sort of eye-catching initiative. I've been in schools before where every pupil has their very own iPad with which they can access the lessons directly and save them, as well as drastically reduce the school's carbon footprint through waste paper. In reality all that happens is that the kids end up spending every lesson playing Candy Crush, but still, it's the thought that counts.

The school itself was fairly small and, despite being in one of the most deprived areas of the North West, had managed to consistently maintain a "Good" rating with OFSTED. To put it simply, they did fantastically well with what they were given, sort of like a supermodel from Hull. Somehow attaining conventional beauty despite swimming in what must surely be the shallowest of gene pools.

The interview began with a 20 minute lesson based on a war poem of our choosing. I selected Wilfred Owen's magnificent *Dulce Et Decorum Est* and had a couple of volunteers acting out the poem to demonstrate the physicality of the piece. It was a wonderful idea, and the kids got a kick out of seeing their mates "bent double, like old beggars under sacks, knock-kneed, coughing like hags". The engagement was through the roof and when I left, I heard one pupil go "awww, I liked him."

The face to face interview was much trickier. I remember completely floundering about a question regarding raising boys attainment. I didn't even know what that meant, so I just reeled off as much bullshit as I could think of - "I think, when it comes to raising boys attainment, it's about finding out the reasons boys are failing to attain, and going from there." With verbal diarrhoea like that, at least if teaching didn't work out I could always carve out a semi-successful career in politics.

There were four interviewees in total - along with myself there was a girl who'd spent the entirety of her second placement at the school, one was a stubby older fellow who asked to go to the toilet and never came back like we were some sort of blind date gone horribly wrong, and the final was a woman who'd been working here for a year as an NQT, and had now been made to essentially interview to keep her own job, never a good sign that you're a valued member of staff. She dispatched herself not long after her lesson, coming back to the staff room in a fit of tears and being consoled by a receptionist. I could hear her make out in between sobs "it's not fair" and "I shouldn't have to do this" and perhaps most telling of all "they're fucking bullies."

At this point some red flags should have been recognised, but to be perfectly honest, I'd left finding a job so late she could have told me the place was haunted and it still wouldn't have put me off. After the face to face interview it was between myself and the girl that had been here six months, who all the staff knew, who'd had half a year to show everyone what she was about. I didn't harbour much hope. In fact I was already logging into a teaching app to apply for more jobs when we got called in to the Head's office.

We were each offered a job. We both accepted.

The first person I told was Holly, who was probably even more excited than I was. I had secured a job with roughly two weeks to spare. At the end of the course we had a small party, and I found out I was the last person to secure a job. "We all thought you were going to drop out!" Said Chelsea, the Science teacher cum TOWIE extra.

In fact, of all the people that started the course, every single one of us made it through to the end, admittedly some more easily than others.

Anna had secured a role early on in the process, and was joining one of the most prestigious academies in the area. She even handed out business cards to each of us. Business cards at a fucking *party*. Christ, never go to a rave with her. She'd probably be on the dance floor doing a presentation. Andrea had been offered a role at the school where she'd been a teaching assistant for so many years. Saima had accepted a role teaching English in Kazakhstan, where she could expect a starting salary of £70,000 tax free, a fully paid house on a private compound, a company car, and three flights home paid for per year. If they'd had a burgeoning stand up comedy scene in Kazakhstan I'd have probably joined her. Teach during the day, joke about Genghis Khan at night.

I felt indebted to Moorfields, and in a way I still do. Without them, I wouldn't have passed the course. It was only through them that I knew how great teaching could be, and without that knowledge I'd have assumed my experience at St Matthews was the standard. Moorfields taught me to be brave with my lessons, to take risks, and to never settle for the monotony that overcomes so many dead-behind-the-eyes educators. Such was their commitment to pushing boundaries, on the day that I left an assistant headteacher was teaching a full class by using Virtual Reality headsets. You turn up to St Matthews with a VR headset and they'd probably call them the devil's goggles and burn them in a bin outside, dousing them with holy water and reading psalms to ward away the evil spirits.

Course leaders from other schools had been invited and, one by one, came up and gave a short and informal speech about what the profession meant to them. Linda spoke about how teaching had given her life purpose and meaning. Margaret, never one to sugar coat things, spoke about how difficult the job was. "The hardest part for me," she said, captivating the room with her spellbinding unassuming nature, "is having a child call you every name under the sun, the worst things imaginable, and tomorrow morning having to wipe the slate clean. There are no grudges. No vendettas. You have to wake up the next day having forgiven everything, and give them another chance to get it right."

Margaret retired from teaching at the end of the year, and Moorfields lost it's most cherished kin. She left behind a legacy spanning four decades, touching the lives of tens of thousands of children in the area, and inspiring the staff around her. On her final day, hundreds of members of the community came by to applaud her as she left the premises for one last time. Children who she currently taught stood shoulder to shoulder with their parents who'd also had the pleasure of being taught by her - a loss felt over generations. Not a bad way to bow out.

CHAPTER 15

"Here's the door code in case you want to come in during the holidays and redecorate your classroom" said the receptionist at Fairhaven Technology College, which will henceforth be referred to only as Fairhaven to stop me having to type out two extra redundant words every time. At first I thought she was joking - expecting me to come in and perform some sort of DIY makeover like a special episode of one of those home renovation programmes. Perhaps I could rope in some extra help - get Lawrence Llewelyn-Bowen to fashion some velveteen drapes, maybe see if Alan Titchmarsh fancies coming round with some potted geraniums, or we could rope Nick Knowles in to come down and do whatever the hell it is that he supposedly does.

Alas, this is something entirely expected of teachers in the modern day. We are a Swiss Army knife, expected to not only be educators but also councillors, activity coordinators, after school club runners, bake sale enthusiasts, charity workers, and now painter and decorators. In no other job would this be an acceptable request for an employee - imagine working as an accountant, taking two weeks annual leave, and then getting a phone call telling you to come in and re-tile the men's toilets.

I decided to come in early and get it out of the way - I spent roughly half a day printing things off and stapling them to walls. I left the biggest wall blank and decided that if anyone asked, that was going to be dedicated to the work of the pupils. I figured nobody was going to question it, and carried on randomly sticking verbs on the wall. By the time I'd finished my classroom looked like someone had ripped pages out of an oversized dictionary and staged a dirty protest, a collection of random words interspersed with general shit.

When I arrived back at the school six weeks later after the end of the summer half term, I was in for a rude awakening. Before the new school year officially started, there was a staff INSET day to help welcome those new to the school and to give each department a chance to familiarize themselves with one another. The modern school has an increasingly high turnover of staff. Much like a football team, staff will often move around schools every few years to progress their careers and move higher up the pay scale. Gone are the days of the one-club teacher, trained in the academy and spending the entirety of an illustrious career in the same place. In fact, some interviewers even take being in one school in a negative light. To some, it shows you've 'settled' - prospective schools would rather see an array of different schools on there as it demonstrates your ability to acclimatize, and there's a theory you'll have been exposed to more ideas and practices and thus be more innovative yourself.

To those not involved in teaching, staff INSET days look like an excuse for teachers to spend a day in their own clothes, arseing about and commenting on how much better their workplace is without the thousand or so mini-human-wrecking-balls inhabiting it. In reality, the staff INSET day is one long gruelling meeting, and most of us would rather be actually teaching than sitting in a freezing sports hall listening to some higher management prick witter on about the importance of setting high expectations.

Teaching is constantly evolving and re-evaluating. What was considered best practice ten years ago is now seen as antiquated, and teaching from twenty years ago would probably get you sacked in the present day. As I arrived at Fairhaven, the zeitgeist was "Growth Mindset", and thus half of the day was spent prattling on about what a "Growth Mindset" is (which can essentially be summed up in three words, "don't give up") and how to foster one in the children we teach.

The second half of the INSET consisted of what can best be

described as a tactical briefing among the new intake of Year 7s, followed by some time to acquaint ourselves with our departments. When a new crop of children arrive at a school, the information passed from their primary schools is collated and analysed and we look for potential child geniuses and child criminals. Said information varies vastly in quality - some primaries send across detailed dossiers containing everything about a pupil down to their fingerprints and DNA, others send across a sentence or two and leave you to figure out the rest for yourself.

No matter what your primary school might say, kids arrive at their secondaries with a reputation. Whether they live up to it or not is very much up to them. During the briefing we were told to pay close attention to two new arrivals - Catherine and Declan. The former had accused two male teachers on two separate occasions of inappropriately touching her, allegations which were found to be false by nothing more than the sheer luck of being caught on CCTV at the time.

Catherine had been given lots of time with a child psychologist, who uncovered a history of sexual abuse from a family friend. Whilst Catherine had shown progress and not made any false allegations in over a year, it was decided that no male members of staff should be left alone with her at any time. We were reminded that, should any accusation be made, we would be suspended indefinitely pending an investigation. She is not, we were told, a malicious child, rather one with an intense craving for attention who has uncovered a rather sinister way of getting it and is unaware of the consequences behind her actions.

Declan, on the other hand, was pitched to us as Satan incarnate. His rap sheet had more raps than a Kanye West album. He cursed like a sailor, got expelled for starting a fire, and was in so many fights he had to have his break and lunch in a special isolated room. I half expected him to turn up on the first day of school like Hannibal Lecter, tied to a metal girder with a mask around his mouth, gurgling and spitting like a broken tap.

And luckily for me, I was to be his English teacher. It felt a bit like being told you had to teach sign language to Ted Bundy, or give Jeffrey Dahmer clarinet lessons.

After lunch we were afforded time with our new departments. With the experience from St Matthews still freshly ringing in my ears, I would do anything to make a good first impression. The Head of Department, Nina, was someone I'd recognised from my interview. She had jet black hair tied tightly in a bun and wore a pair of rectangular glasses, also black. She wore a black pantsuit and her shirt was a very dark shade of grey, clearly adding some much needed colour to the outfit. She looked like a funeral director, and spoke in the same sombre tone.

"As you can tell we've got some new faces, so let's say hello to Freddy and Lauren." She said, her voice dragging on every vowel like a skateboard going through a swamp. "Lauren I'm sure we all remember from her time here on the PGCE course last year, but Freddy's brand new, and he's the only male in the department!" This wasn't something I'd even clocked, but apparently I was the first male member of the English department here in about ten years. It didn't seem like a big deal to me, but Nina made it out like I was some sort of genetic wonder, like I could fly or something.

The women in the department let out a collective "ooooh" as though I was being introduced as the stripper for a hen party rather than a new member of staff. I wasn't too bothered about being objectified in this way - I'm an 18 stone balding bearded man. If your love life is so baron that you'll stoop so low as to sexualise me, it's you I pity more than anything.

We began by finalising the curriculum for the coming year and going over what literature we were going to be teaching, our timetables were then assigned to us and we were ushered away into our classrooms to make sure we had enough supplies for the term ahead. Since Lauren and I were new, Nina escorted us to our classrooms personally, which were conveniently located opposite from one another.

Walking into Lauren's classroom made me feel like Charlie Bucket walking into Willy Wonka's chocolate factory for the first time. The place was wondrous. The displays were breathtaking, some were interactive, and most incredibly of all there was a tree in the corner of the room that she had fashioned from ripping apart old books. Her inventiveness and creativity shone through the room. Hell, the classroom was better decorated than my apartment. Nina was impressed, gushing over Lauren's interior design skills. The standard was set, the bar was high, and when Nina brought me to my room and opened the door, her expectations came crashing down. "Oh," she said, "did you not manage to decorate yours?"

As I walked up to the gates of Fairhaven for the first time as a member of staff, I got the familiar twinges of nervous energy you get whenever you're in a new school. Even as someone who's nerves have been dulled by years of performances, you still feel a degree of apprehension that is to be expected when thrusting yourself into new surroundings. The pressure of having to establish myself yet again was at the forefront of my mind, and I needed to hit the ground running so that the pupils and staff respected me.

I'd been through this ritual twice before over the last twelve months, so I knew roughly what to expect. What I wasn't prepared for though was just how different teaching a class on your own feels compared to having someone else in the room. The best way to describe it is by comparing it to passing your driving test. When taking driving lessons, you become accustomed to having an instructor in your car; telling you what to do and where to go, reassuring you when you're lacking confidence and correcting you when you're doing something wrong. After you pass your test, you suddenly have to get used to not having that reassuring voice sat next to. On the one hand, it's freeing. You are truly the master of your own destiny. On the other, you become acutely aware of having total responsibility. Run a red light? Your fault. Accidentally speeding? Your fault. Crash the car into a ditch? Your fault.

It is often said that once you pass your test and go out on the road alone is only when you really learn how to drive. The same can be said for teaching. Once you experience the feeling of being solely responsible for a classes education do you really begin to experience the pressures, the emotions, the frustrations and the elations that come part and parcel with this most unique of professions.

There's an old saying amongst teachers when it comes to marking their territory at a new school

- "don't smile until Easter." The theory goes that it's far easier to portray an image of a tyrannical disciplinarian and then soften up over time as the kids realise you're not to be fucked with, than it is to come across as a friendly affable pushover and then gradually become more strict if the kids don't respect you.

Education is full of these truisms, words of wisdom handed down from generation to generation, the immovable axioms on which we build our understanding of the job. One piece of advice I was given was, when interviewing for a new school, always look for how many kids are wearing trainers. The more students in trainers, the worse the school is. It's not an exact science by any means but there is *some* validity to this - schools with more stringent uniform policies almost always have a higher level of behaviour amongst the pupils.

This is, in a nutshell, why many pupils have such a hard line on uniform and appearance. The thinking behind it is that teenagers will always rebel against something, all you can do is set the battlegrounds. Far better they rebel with short skirts and eyeliner and shirts untucked than by vandalising property and being genuinely disruptive.

My first day at Fairhaven was relatively uneventful - the pupils were relatively well behaved as they were preoccupied with sussing me out and figuring what they could and couldn't get away with under my stewardship, and I in turn was treading carefully around them, giving little of myself away. Monday played out like the opening moves of a chess match, deliberate and cautionary, with neither side wanting to test the other's patience.

This temporary stand-off gave me chance to familiarise myself with the culture at Fairhaven, certainly a world away from St Matthews. Back again were the hour long lessons, thank God, but strangely enough form class was at the end of the day rather than the beginning. This is highly irregular - most schools choose to have form at the beginning of the day, and it serves rather like a holding pen for cattle. Form time is basically making sure all the kids are in the school by the time lessons actually start, and for relaying any important messages across to the students. I soon found out that the reason Fairhaven moved their form time to the end of the day was to stop the children doing a runner after lunch.

Fairhaven was full of peculiarities - but rather than their origins be shrouded in mystery like at St Matthews ("it's just the St Matthews way!"), the rationale behind everything was clearly explained. For example, Fairhaven had its own on-site laundry room. This was because a frightening proportion of the children here were from backgrounds where washing a school uniform wasn't always possible. This could either be because they couldn't afford a washer themselves, or their gas and electric had been switched off at homes, or perhaps most heartbreakingly of all, their carers were neglectful enough to not consider clean clothes to be important.

There are many sobering images you see as a teacher, but the sight of a queue of children on a Monday morning all waiting to get their clothes washed is one that will stay with me for a long time. Furthermore, Fairhaven gave out free breakfasts to everyone in school by 8.15am. This was to encourage pupils to get to school on time, but also to make sure they had access to a breakfast, a luxury which seldom students did at home.

If the St Matthews way was to cherry pick the best children and have weird rules for no discernible reason, the Fairhaven way was to take some of the most socio-economically disadvantaged children in the country and to level the playing field by giving them access to the things most kids take for granted.

This was made possible in no small part thanks to the monumental efforts of the headteacher, Mrs Morley.

Standing at a shade over five foot, with thinning blonde hair and a voice that always felt strained when pushed over a whisper, Mrs Morley was never going to be the Trunchbull-esque dictator we like to characterise headmistresses as. Instead she was more like Bo Peep; a gentle and supportive shepherdess that doted on her flock selflessly. She was well aware of the background most of these children came from, the abuse that many had to put up with at home, she therefore worked tirelessly on making her school a respite from all that.

The staff at Fairhaven revered Mrs Morley with God-like status, for she went to great lengths to be as accommodating as possible in every regard. Too often school teachers feel pressure not just from parents, but from upper management, and they are squeezed into little quivering balls of stress. Mrs Morley took a different approach - she knew everyone at this school would have their hands full managing their classrooms, and as far as she was concerned, we already had enough on our plate without her adding to our worries.

Such an outlook is incredibly rare among Heads, but is always appreciated.

On my first day at Fairhaven, I thought I'd hit the jackpot. An incredibly supportive school and kids that were no worse than what I was used to in terms of behaviour. On the second day, I realised just how wrong I was.

CHAPTER 16

It took me all of 24 hours at Fairhaven to gain a nickname with the children. Most teachers have nicknames, and most of the time it's just whatever swear word rhymes most with your surname.

Mr Pratt becomes Mr Twatt, Mrs Pratchett becomes Mrs Fat-tits, and so on. Occasionally teachers will garner a moniker that's more focused on their physical appearance - I once worked with a P.E teacher who the students all called "Pidgey", when I asked why he was called Pidgey they told me it was short for pigeon, because he had a remarkably small head. Once they pointed it out, I could no longer unsee it. Teenagers are excellent at sniffing out your biggest insecurities and using them against you.

My nickname, I discovered pretty quickly, was Hagrid. I was quite happy with that to be honest. I'm big, I'm bearded, I teach English and this was a character from a book, I could have no complaints. Besides, who doesn't love a bit of Robbie Coltrane. The way I found out my nickname was from intercepting a note in class. I saw a bit of paper being passed about and children giggling, and with a deftness Margaret herself would have been proud of, I promptly intercepted the offending parchment. I probably shouldn't have looked at what it said though - for when I unfolded it I saw the words "You're a wizard, Harry."

That afternoon I was teaching Declan, the boy we had been warned about during the meeting. At the beginning of the day, I was copied into an email chain with some other staff being given a further heads up about Declan and what we had learned about him on his first day. Declan, apparently, seemed to respond best to a shit ton of praise, but was incredibly defensive if he felt he'd done something wrong. The email therefore suggested a gentle approach full of encouragement.

When Declan's class came in, they were a typical bunch of Year 7s, bright eyed and bushy tailed and eager to impress. When I called Declan's name on the register, I made sure to look up so I could put a face to a name. When I caught sight of him, he was nothing at all like I'd expected.

He was maybe the smallest child in the class, with a mop of shaggy blonde hair and twinkling blue eyes. He looked like butter wouldn't melt. During the first 15 minutes, he was as good as gold. He put his hand up to answer questions, listened intently, and seemed as keen as anyone to put in a good impression.
I asked two students to hand the books out, Declan put his hand up,

but I chose some children closer to the front. I didn't note his immediate reaction, but he can't have taken it particularly well, as he waited for a pupil to come to his desk with his book and stabbed them in the leg with a biro. The child yelped like he'd just been shot, and before I could say anything, Declan looked at me and went "What?" As if he somehow had a right to feel hard done by.

Remembering the advice from the email, I took a soft approach instead of screaming and shouting. "Now Declan," I said in as diplomatic a way as I could muster, "that's not an appropriate thing to do to someone, is it?"

"Fuck off."

This was the first time a student had sworn directly at me. I knew the day would come eventually, I just didn't think I'd pop my swear cherry to a 12 year old miniature member of the Hitler Youth. I tried to regain my composure - "Excuse me?!" I replied.

"You heard me," responded Declan, getting out of his chair and quite literally squaring up to me, "go and fuck yourself you fat cunt."

Fat cunt? Wow. I preferred Hagrid.
As I stood there, dumbfounded, wondering whether or not battering

a child would get me prison time, Declan decided to boot me as hard as he could in the shin. It didn't hurt very much, the only thing bruised was my pride. I marched him right down to his Head of Year's office and left him there.

Declan lasted less than a week in mainstream education, and to be honest, most of us were surprised he made it that far. After the first day, the novelty of school had well and truly worn off for him and he seemed to challenge himself to cause as much disruption as humanly possible. On his third day, he went up to the biggest kid in Year 11 (a county rugby player) and punched him square in the balls. My only thinking is that he'd seen one too many prison films and thought the way to control the yard was by beating the shit out of the biggest person he could find and hope everyone else would fall in line.

On Friday afternoon myself and the rest of Declan's teachers were called into a meeting with the school safeguarding officer. Every school by law has a safeguarding officer - usually it's a non-teaching member of staff whose job it is to look after child welfare. Anything suspicious about a child, from bruises to sexualised behaviour, you are trained to pass onto your safeguarding officer. Much better it turns out to be nothing and you've just bothered them unnecessarily than it to be the warning signs of grooming or abuse that you failed to pass on.

The safeguarding officer thanked us all for dealing with Declan. I was by no means the only one he accosted. When a French teacher asked him to speak French, he spat at her. When Mr Ahmed, a maths teacher, told him to stop shouting out during class, he began shouting every racial slur under the sun at him, sort of like a Britain First member with Tourette's. Kicking my leg seemed tame in comparison. In fact, had we been told he was staying at the school, I'd have probably just gone out and bought some shinpads. Problem solved.

Instead, the safeguarding officer told us that Declan would not be rejoining us. Unfortunately, Declan had lived a short and yet immensely troubled life. His mother gave him up for adoption after his father had done a runner. The next ten years had been spent being passed around from pillar to post in the adoption system, but last year Declan had finally found a foster family that he connected with and had made some real progress. Over the summer holidays Declan's birth mother had decided she wanted to "reconnect" with her son. After a month she asked Declan to leave his foster family and come back to live with her, and naturally the prospect of having his 'real' mum back wasn't something Declan could turn down.
It took all of a fortnight before Declan's mum decided she didn't

want him again, which happened to coincide with him going back to school. Maybe the prospect of waking him up every morning, making his sandwiches, ensuring he's got the right equipment and all the other things a parent is supposed to do just felt like too much of a responsibility. Once again she denounced ownership, and once again Declan was thrust back into the adoption system. Sadly, Declan couldn't just go back to the foster family he'd connected with - it doesn't work like that. This time he was leaving the area completely for a family in Leeds that were willing to take him in.

The first week at a new school is a stressful time for any child. Declan was dealing with this, plus having to sleep on his grandparents couch after his mother had abandoned him for the second time in his life, knowing he'd given up the only family he'd ever felt comfortable around just to be with her again. It was heartbreaking to hear, and it put everything in perspective. With all of that going on in his life, the fact he'd even made it into school to begin with was an achievement considering those circumstances. And there we all were, thinking we'd been hard done by, because we'd been kicked or sworn at or spat at. I learned another lesson about teaching then and there - never judge a book by it's cover.

The pace at Fairhaven was relentless. Circumstances could change in the blink of an eye. There were so many pupils with so many issues, we needed weekly meetings to track all the new developments. The key to behaviour management at Fairhaven was staying one step ahead, often it felt like we were one step behind. A teenage criminal mind is a hive of ingenuity, and the more we as teachers stepped up our attempts to stamp out their misdeeds, the more creative they became in disguising them.

There were, for example, several Year 11 girls who decided to go out and get tongue piercings (a school no-no). They initially tried to hide it, but hiding a tongue piercing is a bit like trying to hide three golf balls in your mouth at once. Even if you keep your mouth shut, we can still see the lumps. The girls, faced with a period in isolation, decided the best course of defence would be to tell their teachers that, rather than having a fashion accessory stabbed in their mouths, that they had root canal surgery instead. The probability of having nine girls from the same year and friendship group all having extensive dental work over the same weekend notwithstanding, some poor member of staff still had to phone home and check.

Phoning home was always a part of the job I absolutely dreaded, because truth be told you never knew what was on the other end of the line. Some parents could not be more supportive and would probably go as far as to let you cane their child if it meant getting them their GCSEs. Other parents took any criticism of their child personally, as though they were being chastised for bad parenting. One time I had to ring home as a child kept coming in with trainers on whilst having his real school shoes in his bag. He'd leave the house with his school shoes, change into his trainers, come to school, then pretend he forgot. His plan was for us to give up and say "remember them tomorrow", but said plan seemed to rely on us forgetting he'd done the same thing every day for about a month. Nevertheless, he'd still be adamant that this time he'd genuinely lost them and they weren't just in his bag. Then after 20 wasted minutes of back and forth, he'd open his bag, and like the whitest magic trick ever, there his shoes were.

After telling the parent of our predicament, he responded with "Well, what do you expect ME to do about it?"

"Could you check his bag before he goes to school? And if his trainers are in there, take them out?"

"What, every fucking day?" He replied, as though checking his son's bag before school was one of the Labours of Hercules. Slay the Nemean lion, clean the Augean stables in a day, take a pair of trainers out of a bag.

Another time I rang home to speak to the parents of a Year 9 boy who was struggling with English. I'd put on extra revision sessions for the class after school, and made attendance mandatory. I rang home the parents personally and thought it would be a fairly easy sell - "Hi, your child's struggling in English, I'm therefore devoting more of my time to teaching them on a more personal basis to ensure they pass, they just need to turn up" - but not every parent responded to my offer of free extra tuition with the gumption I'd anticipated. One even went as far as to tell me "It's not my fault he's fucking thick."

Teenagers with tongue studs and less than supportive parents are a mainstay of most educational institutions, but what made Fairhaven unique was the significant number of pupils who took their misbehaviour to extremities. At the beginning of my second week, every member of staff was sent an email warning them about lifting tables. This was not because they were worried someone might put their back out, rather that some students had taken to sticking razor blades under the tables so that the staff would cut their fingers open when lifting them at the end of the day. One unfortunate caretaker even had to visit A&E for stitches. In the end, a school-wide assembly was called where Mrs Morley told her thousand-or-so pupils that "we know who's doing it, but if you stop now it won't go any further". This was, in no uncertain terms, the bluff of the century. Nobody had the faintest idea who was doing it. They were one of the great unsolved cases and would no doubt secure their own place in history along with other illustrious names - Jack the Ripper, The Zodiac Killer, The Fairhaven Slasher. Thankfully whoever it was got successfully spooked and the issue vanished as quickly as it had appeared.

I wish I could say that was the last time I had an incident with razor blades at Fairhaven, but barely a month into my teaching career at the school and I had the unfortunate experience of having to deal with two Year 9 girls who slit their wrists mid way through my lesson. It does make you wonder just how bad of a teacher you are that suicide was more preferable than spending another twenty minutes learning about A Christmas Carol. There were copious amounts of blood to contend with; this was no nick of the skin, rather an elaborate reenactment of that scene in Carrie. I sent them both out of the class immediately to the on site nurse. In hindsight, I should have asked them to smear their bloody hands over the blank wall at the back of the room so I could tell the Head of Department it was a display themed around Macbeth.

I learned quite early on that disciplining children using traditional methods simply didn't work at Fairhaven. They already had so much shit going on in their lives that you threatening to keep them behind for 15 minutes at lunch really didn't make much of a difference. It would be like threatening the captain of a sinking ship with a cup full of water, demanding he do what you ask or you'll pour it all over the deck.

One behaviour management technique I'd picked up during my training would be to ask pupils to wait outside the classroom and then shout at them in the corridor one-to-one. Most unruly students thrive off a captive audience, take that away from them and they are rendered powerless. Another is to casually mention the child's parents - just being reminded of the threat of phoning home can work wonders. I saw this played to perfection once at Moorfields; a Year 8 child was severely disrupting the lesson and the teacher, calm as you like, walked over to him with a sticky note. She passed the note to the child and simply said "just checking that's the right number?" It was the pupil's home telephone number. He went as white as a sheet. The implication of phoning home was all that was needed.

The most difficult class I taught were my Year 10s. The room was packed full of characters, so much so that no amount of seating plans seemed to make any difference. You couldn't keep the troublesome personalities away from one another, there were simply too many. It was like an unsolvable riddle - how to sit them in such an order so that no two knob heads were sat next to one another.

In one of my first lessons with them, a girl named Evie was disrupting the lesson with her trademark brand of teenage petulance. What I didn't know at the time, because nobody thought to tell me, was that Evie was part of the notorious 'Sordell' family, who'd been sending shitty children to the school for years. Evie was the fourth of five kids who'd attended Fairhaven. The first three were expelled by Year 9. Evie had made it to Year 10 by the skin of her teeth, but she seemingly had no plans to see Year 11.

I told Evie to stop distracting her classmates and threatened her with a detention, to which she took about as much notice as a driver in a high speed police chase would take of a red light. I decided a stronger course of action was needed, and asked her to wait outside the classroom so I could speak to her one-to-one. After a few minutes I joined her in the corridor where, far from looking apprehensive about her impending bollocking, she seemed completely nonplussed by the situation. I began to shout at her but quickly realised there was little point, she was barely listening as it was. Time to bring out the big guns. "By acting in this way, you're disrespecting me as your teacher." I said, laying down the ground rules before delivering the fatal sucker punch. "What if I called home and told them? What would Mum and Dad think?"

Evie paused for a moment. For a second I thought she was holding back tears. In fact, she was perfecting the timing of her own retort.

"Well, my Dad's in prison and my mum's a prostitute and a drug addict, so I don't think they'd mind."

And with that, she walked back into the lesson, as if what she'd said was the most natural thing in the world.

CHAPTER 17

Department meetings were held once a week on a Tuesday at 4pm. Chaired by Nina, the Head of English, they were a chance for her to touch base with us about problems the department was facing and potential issues on the horizon. Here we discussed everything from full schemes of work to individual pupils. The idea was to have a proactive approach and to increase transparency, since we'd be in contact on a regular basis.

The reality was far different. Nina was not the type of boss to remain cool and level headed during a crisis. In her eyes, if there was a problem, it was because someone fucked up. Thus the weekly departmental meetings were often a torturous hour of Nina asking if there were any problems, and everyone flat out denying they had any problems, despite there being lots and lots and lots of problems. You quickly learned that if you had an issue, you had one of two choices. Either raise it with Nina and she'll shout at you and leave you to solve the problem yourself, or hope Nina doesn't find out about it before you've fixed whatever's gone wrong and save yourself a bollocking. Everyone chose the latter.

Nina might have been bullish, but she wasn't naive. She knew there were challenges, and resented them being kept from her. So all the English staff had to play out this bizarre little dance, a pantomime of deception, where we'd all be covering our own arses whilst Nina sniffed around looking for the problems we were keeping from her. Inevitably this led to some people covering for others and alliances and friendships being forged off the back of it, and over time these alliances became inter-departmental cliques.

On the face of it, cliques get a bad rap. There's nothing wrong with certain members of staff deciding they have more in common and forming their own friendship bubble, providing of course they still maintain accommodating to those they have to work with. But, like milk from the shop in a petrol station, they can turn sour very quickly.

At Fairhaven's English department a clique had formed between Zoe, a fiery red-headed teacher who was the Deputy Head of Department and bore a stunning resemblance to Little Mai from The Moomins, a passive aggressive woman named Angela, a part-time teacher called Marie (I once called her Maria by mistake and she shot daggers at me for a month), and the newest addition Lauren, the girl I had my interview with. That left three members of the department that weren't in the clique, the Head of

Department Nina, a jolly Sikh woman named Alina, and myself.

The clique's main priority was self-preservation. They worked together to hoard resources and equipment. In a school as deprived of funding as Fairhaven, even basics like pens and paper were scarce. Items like board markers were rarer still - in fact most teachers bought whiteboard markers themselves, it was just easier than having to go on a scavenger hunt every couple of weeks. But they also protected themselves from the wrath of Nina; they knew she was constantly searching for problems in her department and had learned to manage this by pushing her attention onto other members of staff.

This is what the woman in the interview had meant when she'd said "they're all fucking bullies." It turned out the clique had spent so much time trying to make Nina believe all the department's problems stemmed from this one woman that the Head of Department had decided to make her re-interview for her own job. And they hired me instead.

I wish I could say I figured all this out on my own, but for the first couple of weeks I remained completely oblivious to it. It was only after Alina pulled me to one side to give me fair warning did I see things for what they truly were. Alina had been at the school for many years. During that time she'd watched the clique form and develop, and initially it was her that bore the brunt of their meddling. Things got so bad that Alina contacted her union rep and, after much negotiation and back and forth, things eventually settled down. The experience of being targeted had strangely brought Alina and Nina quite close together, and while Alina and the clique were technically at peace with one another, an underlying tension had remained ever since, occasionally manifesting through passive aggressive pleasantries exchanged in the staff room.

Have you ever not noticed something until it was pointed out to you, and then it suddenly changes how you perceive that thing to the point where you can barely see past what you once

overlooked? That's what working with the clique was like. For starters, they were never far apart from one another. They were pack animals. Secondly, they never seemed to lack resources or books, and if you were to ask for some of their stuff they'd inevitably find a reason to not have to give it to you. Also, because of Zoe's connections as the deputy Head of Department, the clique were given advance warning on all the happenings in school. If something was afoot, they'd planned for it and worked out how to commandeer the necessary equipment for it before I'd even heard about it. One time Nina revealed the book Year 8's would be studying for the year, and each one of the clique had conveniently already procured a stash of the novels in each of their classrooms. They were impossible to outmanoeuvre, they were so well connected. It was like Fairhaven had its own version of the Mafia, four young women dealing school supplies like they were contraband.

Nina, for her part, knew about the clique. She may have been unaware how well they manipulated her, but she knew there were certain members of her department that served each other's interests before anyone else's. However, there wasn't an awful lot she could do about it, and that's even if she wanted to get involved in the first place. It was far easier for Nina to turn a blind eye and let them get away with it. Alina warned me that the clique would target me because I was new and naive to the politics of the department. At first I vowed to keep a low profile, not to piss anyone off, and to rise above the inter-departmental power struggle. But it wasn't long before the clique had my demise set firmly in their sights.

Mid-way through October Zoe swung by my classroom. She made an audible sigh as she glanced around the room and saw the big wall at the back of the room, still empty of decoration. "I just wanted to make you aware," said Zoe, "that we're transferring a pupil into your Year 10 class. She was with Lauren but she's, erm, not settling in well there. We think it might be because she's actually too smart for that class and she's not feeling challenged, so we're moving her up to your Year 10 class."

There wasn't even the slightest of hints that I might have a choice in the matter. The pupil in question was a girl named Kayla, and despite having never taught her myself I was well aware of her reputation as one of the most troublesome pupils in school. When I told Alina about it, she was outraged. "That's fucking bollocks. She's too thick for the set she's in at the moment. But Zoe teaches the set below and she's not going to have her, so they've moved her with you. Did they at least take one of your kids off you in exchange?"

I shook my head.

"That's fucking bollocks" Alina repeated again in what was quickly becoming her new catchphrase. In Alina's opinion, the very least Zoe could have done would be to offer me the
chance to trade out one of my most troublesome pupils in return, sort of like an organised swap meet to keep your class dickhead count from increasing.

I had a week's notice to prepare for Kayla's arrival, because she was currently serving her second three-week long suspension of the school year. This was especially impressive considering we
were six weeks and two days into said school year. Her first

suspension had been for calling an assistant headteacher a "scruffy cunt" and then running away when he tried to reprimand her.

The second suspension happened on her first day back at the beginning of her first lesson. You'd think that after being kicked out of school for almost a month one would endeavour to keep a low profile, not Kayla. She waited until her name had been taken on the register, walked straight up to a girl she didn't get along with and head butted her square in the face. Another three week suspension.

You'd be forgiven for wondering what the hell you'd have to do to get a permanent expulsion at Fairhaven. At any school, expulsions are a last resort. There are several things we try first, such as engaging with the parents or guardians of the pupil to see if we can work together to change behaviour patterns. Unfortunately, Kayla's mum was basically an older version of Kayla. I had the pleasure of meeting her once, she looked like Boris Johnson crossed with Vicky Pollard. She was in the school reception, quite literally screaming her head off, because she'd parked outside the school the day before on double yellow lines and received a parking ticket. Despite the fact that there are numerous signs saying not to park there and that the school does not have anything to do with the traffic wardens patrolling the area, she wanted the school to pay the fine. When the school refused and told her to contact the council, she threw a tantrum and was escorted off premises. I think she must have thought all public services were interchangeable, and the people teaching her children also did her bin collections and filled in potholes in the street.

Since Kayla's mother was a borderline psychopath, engaging her in disciplining her daughter was a non-starter. In fact if anything, she regularly took Kayla's side. The next step was a managed move, which is when schools partner up and swap the worst kids with one another for a few weeks. You take one of mine, I'll take one of yours. Kind of like when hostile countries swap prisoners with one another.

Managed moves have a fairly low long term success rate, but they're always worth a try. When a difficult pupil moves school, they are taken completely out of their comfort zone and go from being in classes with all of their friends to being surrounded by people they don't know in a building they get lost in. They regress back to that scared little Year 7 on their first day, and that usually curtails their mischievousness . They come back to their original school with a renewed appreciation which translates into better behaviour, or so the theory goes. Sadly what usually happens is any epiphanies about how much better it is at their current school are short lived, and usually they revert back to being little shitbags within a couple of weeks.

Kayla had been on three managed moves. Each one to no avail. The only thing left for her now was expulsion. There was just one thing stopping the school getting rid of her for good - the cost. To expel Kayla on a permanent basis would cost Fairhaven about two grand, money the school could ill afford. When money is so tight that you're counting every penny and there's not enough basic equipment to go around, it was an expense the school simply couldn't justify. It was easier (and cheaper) to keep expelling Kayla for three weeks at a time until she either at the end of Year 11 or just stopped going in altogether. Maybe we could paint double yellow lines on all the streets within a mile radius of the school and hope her mother's too afraid to drop her off.

Now this problem pupil who'd been passed from pillar to post, had just moved up a set into my class despite the notable disadvantage of being unable to stay in school longer than a day without being suspended. The clique had once again come through for their own at the expense of everyone else. I'd have to find a way to incorporate her into what was already a very demanding class.

I made an extra special effort to get along with Kayla, but my God, she fucking hated me. From the moment we laid eyes on each other, we mixed about as well as oil and water. Our personalities contrasted more than the horrendous orange foundation line on the side of her neck. She was a spoiled brat, intent on getting her own way with everything. She was the type of student that *demanded* your respect, but showed you absolutely none back in return. In short, she was an extreme caricature of a moody, tempestuous, teenage girl.

I'd had relative success with difficult pupils in all of my previous schools, and in fact even at Fairhaven I was developing a reputation as someone that the kids quite liked. The way I achieved this was by treating them like they were adults, not getting angry, letting them make their own choices and making them aware of the consequences. Instead of keeping a child behind after

class to shout at them for not doing their homework, I'd sit down and ask them what we can do to make sure it didn't happen again. I'd let them come up with their own solution. This seemed to work well at Fairhaven, as the majority of kids appreciated just being listened to. This approach, however, did not work with Kayla. The first time I kept her behind, she stuffed her fingers in her ears and hummed until I stopped talking. It's rather tricky to treat someone like an adult when they're going out of their way to act like a fucking baby.

When Kayla walked into my classroom after transferring to my set, she had a hissy fit because she wanted to sit next to her friend (in a seat another pupil was already sitting in) and not at the front next to me. I politely explained that this was the only space available. After ten minutes worth of back and forth she eventually relented, but before I had a chance to celebrate my victory she called me a "fat bastard" under her breath, just loud enough so that the class could hear but quietly enough to deny it if I challenged her. Immediately my comedy instincts kicked in, and I had to stop myself from turning round and saying "at least I don't look like a prostitute oompa loompa."

Instead I simply replied "most people just call me Hagrid."

After every single lesson with Kayla I had to remind myself about Margaret's words of advice on our final day of trainees, about how every night you have to go home and wipe the slate clean and come in the next morning with no grudges or baggage, and give them another chance to get it right. Easier said than done.

CHAPTER 18.

The more time I spent at Fairhaven, the more I felt a deep affinity for the place and everything they were trying to do. My admiration for the headteacher, Mrs Morley, was astronomical. Here she was, captain of a small ship with holes in the vessel and not enough tape to patch them all up, leading a crew of a thousand misfits and ne'er do wells through atrociously stormy seas and not only getting through without capsizing, but without so much as a worried glance. Mrs Morley was unflappable, and it made me feel unflappable too.

After the October half term, I witnessed first hand one of the more challenging aspects about life at Fairhaven. The school holiday had been just two weeks long, but I was shocked at how much weight some pupils had lost. The bones in their faces stuck out more, their skin looked like pale putty, they barely resembled the children that had left a fortnight earlier. At first, I assumed a boy in my Year 11 class may have developed a drug addiction. When I brought it up with the safeguarding officer she told me that it's not uncommon for some of the children to spend the whole half term eating nothing but bread. Call me fanatical, but I'm of the opinion that no child should be brought up with the same diet as a pond full of ducks.

Many children came back malnourished, and some looked like they were starving. The first time you see it, the shock overwhelms you. And the worst part is the looks on the children's faces.

They look embarrassed. Like you might know a secret they never wanted anyone to find out about. Actually, that's not the worst part - the very worst part is quickly it all becomes *normal*.

You start to expect it after every half term, and it makes you feel guilty for having school holidays in the first place.

When you teach children from disadvantaged backgrounds, it's not just having to deal with them not having the right equipment, or having to feed them or wash their clothes, their whole lives are fundamentally altered by their socio-economic circumstances. They experience the world differently to other pupils, and as such you have to reevaluate your approach to teaching them. Is it fair to constantly dish out detentions for no homework for a child that doesn't have access to the internet? Should you punish a kid for turning up late for school every day when they live several miles away and can't afford public transport? You have to make allowances.

Of course, it's not always easy to accommodate pupils in this way. Whilst teaching creative writing to a Year 8 class, I told them that their end of module assessment would be on a description of the beach. "But Sir" one kid at the back put his hand up, "what if we've never been to the beach?"

I asked who in the class had never been to a beach before. About a third raised their hands. I suspect there were probably more. I briefly thought about changing the end of term assignment to 'theme park' but figured if a child hadn't been to the seaside it's fair to assume they've probably not been to Alton Towers either. In the end we changed it to describing a storm. The way I saw it, rich or poor, if you live in England you've probably experienced shitty weather.

Two days before the test a new child got transferred to the school and was lumped in my English class. You'd think that having a new pupil would be worthy of a heads up, but sadly nobody thought to even send me an email. It was like a surprise package - an extra body in the room, an extra book to mark, an extra thing to manage and look after and be responsible for. Thank you so much, no really, *you shouldn't have.*

The kid looked just as surprised to be there as I was. He was a heavy set young man, practically bursting out of his uniform, with a mane of untamed bushy hair. There was no documentation for him, the kids didn't know him, he was just, there. I had to make a judgement call on whether or not this was a legitimate student or a man disguised as a child for free education. I asked his name and found him a seat. "My name is Wilson" he said in a thick accent I couldn't quite place.

Ploughing on with the lesson, the class were preparing for their creative writing test on "The Storm". I had planned a sensory lesson, where we dimmed the lights and listened to the sounds a storm made and made notes, then we watched videos of storms and again made notes on great words and phrases we could use in our essays. I didn't want any child to not know what a storm was like, in the same way they didn't know about beaches or theme parks. This lesson was about levelling the playing field.

No sooner do I turn off all the lights and play storm noises, the new kid Wilson runs out of the room crying his eyes out. It turned out that Wilson had arrived in the UK just a few days ago from his home country of Haiti. He moved to this country because his house got destroyed by a hurricane. No wonder he'd ran out of the room, I'd damn near given the poor lad PTSD.

If I wanted any more evidence of the divide between the have's and the have-not's, my first parent's evening at Fairhaven gave me a front row seat to witness first hand the difference in backgrounds between these kids and the ones I'd taught at St Matthews. For starters, roughly a third of the parents didn't even show up. I'm sure some had legitimate reasons such as work or childcare, but the overwhelming majority just couldn't be bothered. In fact, when I rang home to speak to the parents (a courtesy that cost me two lunch breaks and two hours staying behind after school to complete) one or two of the parents even told me they couldn't be bothered down the phone. If anything they seemed pretty aggrieved that I'd called them and they had to fish their mobile phones out of their pockets and move their mouths to speak to me. It's not too much of a stretch to say that if the parent adopts a couldn't-care-less attitude to education then the child is going to mirror that.

Of the parents that did turn up, it would have been nice to see some proper pants, some trainers, perhaps a shirt if we were feeling especially adventurous. The amount of adults in grey jogging bottoms was absurd. At St Matthews, parents dressed up for parents evening in at least some smart casual attire. They wanted to make a good impression. At Fairhaven the parents' evenings looked like a fashion show for Sports Direct.

The attitude of the parents varied greatly - at St Matthews it was like a business meeting, everything was very formal, it was like doing a script read of Downton Abbey. But at Fairhaven, the relationship between parent and teacher was far more colloquial. One dad even sat down opposite me, shook my hand and said "I've got to say, it's a shame my son's not being taught my Miss Nelson", gesturing to a stunning brunette at the other end of the sports hall.

"Why's that?" I asked.

"Well…. you know……I'd smash that." He replied, more embarrassed for me than anything because he had to *explain* that he wanted to fuck one of my co-workers.

But perhaps the most telling difference between the parents evenings at Fairhaven and at St Matthews were just how few children brought their actual parents. We had a lot of grandparents, aunties, uncles, older siblings, and foster carers. After a while, you stop introducing yourself and asking "are you so-and-so's mum and dad?" Instead you modify your speech ever so slightly to avoid the awkward explanation - "are you the person that looks after so-and-so?"

During the days I'd started spending more and more time with Alina. I'd come by her room and say hello to her every lunchtime just to check in on how her day was going. She was a sweet woman and was generous to a fault. Being able to just talk to her, blow off steam, talk shit about pupils and parents without being judged was so liberating. You couldn't have any of those conversations with anyone else in the department without it being fed back to Nina.

When I'd exhausted all avenues on dealing with Kayla, my most troublesome student, Alina was the one that I turned to. "Why don't you try ignoring her?" She offered. It was different to everything I'd attempted so far; I'd tried being her friend, being her enemy, setting high expectations for her, setting low expectations, having a zero tolerance approach, letting her get away with murder, none of those seemed to have the faintest effect on her gradually depleating behaviour.

The next lesson I had with Kayla, I took Alina's advice and ignored the hell out of her. I paid her about as much attention as a Tory MP gives to starving children during a pandemic. At first, she didn't know what to make of it. She tried interrupting the lesson, tentatively getting out of her seat, all the little tricks in her arsenal that would normally guarantee her some recognition. After a while, the most incredible thing happened. She stopped. It was as though she'd decided there was no longer a game to be played if I was not a willing participant, no dance to be had without a partner.

For the rest of the lesson she was as good as gold, same for the following lesson. I thought I'd cracked teaching. Then she got herself suspended for another three weeks for smoking weed in the school playground. Kayla's mum, rather than being concerned that her 14 year old daughter was taking drugs and could end up with a criminal record, instead decided to shout at the school for taking the marijuana off her when it was 'her property'. In terms of mental gymnastics, even Olympic medallist Simone Biles would have been proud of that somersault.

I could deal with most of the other behavioural issues fine, in fact most of the time I actually found it all quite amusing. When you become a teenager you start to refine your sense of humour, and some kids are genuinely funny little fuckers. You might call it misbehaviour, they'd call it 'banter'. But there's a fine line between the two and there are occasions when a joke can turn into something more serious in the blink of an eye.

My Year 10 class were constantly toeing this tightrope of acceptability with ever greater disregard for the consequences. During a lesson analysing non-fiction texts, I presented the room with two newspaper articles about Emmett Till. Perhaps unsurprisingly, none of them knew who Emmett Till was, so I had to spend five minutes briefly explaining the history of racial tensions in America, Jim Crow laws, and how the attitudes in the north of the country (such as Chicago where Emmett was from) were different from the south (such as Mississippi where the incident took place).

When I'd talked about how Emmett had moved down south recently before a white woman falsely accused him of whistling at her which lead to his trial and death, a slow child at the front of the class called Treyvon exclaimed "Ohhhhhh, so he was a freshy?"

"Yeah, if that helps you to understand it, sure." The pupils seemed more engaged now as I continued explaining. "So this *freshy* comes down from Chicago where the laws are different, and being a *freshy* he's in a new place….." I carried on using the term 'freshy' all lesson whilst the kids giggled away. I didn't mind, laughs meant they were engaged and you can't teach them anything unless they're engaged.

I thought they were laughing because it was funny that a teacher was using slang during a lesson - I was mistaken. It was only once the lesson had ended that Treyvon was kind enough to inform me that 'freshy' meant 'fresh off the boat'.

I'd also grown close to Lauren, the girl I'd interviewed with, but her relationship with the clique meant I was always guarded with what I said around her. I didn't think she was a particularly malicious character, she seemed to love the school with a passion and threw everything into her job, but the company she kept made me keep her at arms length. It's a shame really, when you're in any school you need as many allies as you can get.

Sometimes after a hard day I'd sit back and wonder how all my other coursemates were getting on. I imagined Angela telling a Head of Department somewhere that she could do their job better than them. I thought about Anna, probably crawling so far up a Headteacher's arse she could wear them like a ceremonial hat. I still kept in touch with Saima, she sent me a message telling me that one of her pupils won a national spelling championship and the school gave her an iPad as a thank you present despite the fact she didn't actually do anything. Her pupil had achieved something totally independently to her but she still got an expensive gift anyway.

I text her back "That sounds nice. Today I asked a child to take his coat off and he spat in my face."

CHAPTER 19

Almost every pupil at every school in the country has a form tutor. Or they do at all public schools, anyway. Private schools might be different. Maybe everyone has a butler and there's no need. You simply get Jeeves to inform you of any important school announcements while you make sure there's enough pens in your Gucci pencil case.

As a form tutor, you're responsible for around 30 or so children who you'll see every day. The 15 minutes you spend with them is largely a waste of time, very little gets done, it's just a system for allowing pupils to filter into the school, passing on a few messages, and then allowing them to sit and talk before the school 'officially' starts. Most teachers don't take form seriously at all, they usually just catch up on emails. So much so that it took me until December before I'd bothered to learn everyone's name.

There are some names you'll learn straight away, pupils that are constantly in trouble for one reason for another. One of the first names I learned was Alex - a child with mild autism who'd developed a peculiar coping mechanism for dealing with the stresses of school life. Every time he got into trouble, he'd run away. A teacher would ask him something as innocuous as why he hadn't done his homework and before you could say "The dog ate it" he'd be sprinting down the corridor like Forrest Gump.

Now, in Year 7, this wasn't *too* much of a problem. Sure, it wasn't ideal, but someone would catch up to him and calm him down and the whole thing could be managed. Except Alex never grew out of this habit. By the time he was in Year 10 and puberty had worked it's magic he was running cross country for Lancashire County Council. Fairhaven had to install new gates to
prevent him sprinting off the premises; the old ones were too slow to close and Alex would often slide through them like Indiana Jones in The Temple of Doom. The P.E department had an 'Alex Drill', where they would strategically take up positions on site that allowed them to slowly narrow their search and pin him in. His Head of Year, a keen marathon runner herself, kept a pair of trainers and some leggings in her office just in case she ever needed to join the hunt. As Alex's form tutor, I was sent regular emails detailing his little jaunts. I suggested we just save everyone time and make him wear a Fitbit and I'll just check it at the end of the day.

When you see someone every single day, even if it's just for a quarter of an hour, you begin to be able to recognise changes in their mood and their demeanour. The smallest things becoming blindingly obvious signals that something isn't quite right. Most of the time it's nothing to worry about, they've most likely just had a bad day. Perhaps their alarm didn't go off in the morning, or they missed breakfast, or they left something important at home and got a detention. But occasionally it's the initial warning signs of something more significant, and as a form tutor once you pick up on these things it's your professional obligation to take the pupil to one side and ask if everything's OK.

One day one of the form's biggest personalities, Myley, came in looking sullen, withdrawn and very much at odds with herself. Usually she operated like a cocaine addict with a foghorn, spewing loud nonsense with such ferocity that a fully trained stenographer would struggle to keep up. But today she was muted almost to a whisper, the flickering enthusiasm in her eyes dulled, the puppyish enthusiasm normally exhibited was replaced with a sombreness befitting a bereavement. Naturally I asked her what was wrong, and I was told "nothing".

The following morning Myley came to see me. She carried herself as though the weight of the world was on her shoulders, pushing her down everywhere she went. Myley asked if I remembered yesterday when I asked her if she was OK, I told her I did and asked her again. This time, her answer was different. She wasn't OK. In fact, she was pretty fucking far from OK and she didn't know how to get back to being OK. I told her that the first step would be to tell me what happened and we'd go from there.

She began by telling me about her ex, a boy in the year above. They'd dated for a few months, and against her better judgement, she'd sent him explicit pictures and videos of her which he promised he'd deleted. Surprise surprise, this had turned out not to be the case. In fact, yesterday during a French lesson they shared where the students were allowed on their phones for research, he'd decided it would be a funny idea to send a video of Myley masturbating to everyone in the class.

Naturally the video did the rounds on social media and by lunch everyone had seen it. No wonder by the time I saw her at the end of the day she was so quiet. Imagine being stuck in a building with a thousand people and knowing they're *all* talking about you and they've all seen you in the most explicit ways conceivable. That's not the kind of thing you can cure with a good night's sleep. It's intense psychological trauma inflicted on someone still developing, the kind of thing people can spend years in therapy trying to get over.

I concentrated hard on trying to seem as neutral and unfazed as possible. I didn't want to show any revulsion and make Myley feel even more awkward. At times like this, you have to fight hard to suppress your human instincts, I just wanted to reach out and hug this poor girl and tell her that everything was going to be fine, that the people in her life who really mattered wouldn't think of her any differently, and that the the only think she had to be ashamed of was her atrocious choice in men. But these are times to remember your training and to stay professional. I knew straight away this would be a police matter, and we are told that whenever a child comes to you with an issue such as this that you should write everything down. "If you don't mind, I'm just going to get a pen and paper. My memory's getting worse in my old age" I said, trying to downplay it, but what I was essentially doing was taking a statement.

Once Myley was finished telling me everything that had happened in as much detail as she could account for, I took the paper to her Head of Year, explained what had gone on, and gave her the statement we'd done. The Head of Year promptly called the police, and pulled the boy in question out of lessons. Since I had a free period (my only one of the week), I offered to watch
the boy while the police came. He sat in front of me in an empty room with a deplorable smirk across his face, while I tried to remain

calm and disinterested when really I wanted to jump across the table and beat the living shit out of him.

It riled me how completely unfazed the boy seemed to be. Clearly he couldn't be so thick as to not know what was going on? Perhaps he didn't fully grasp the gravity of the situation, or maybe he thought it was going to be a simple case of her word against his. Either way, it was a hugely satisfying moment to see all of the colour drain from his face the minute the police walked in.

Once the officer told him he was going to take him down to the station and that he was going to have to give a statement with a parent or guardian present, the reality began to set in. "What have I even done though?" The boy asked angrily, trying to mask his nervousness with incredulity.

The police officer calmly responded with three words that left the boy shell-shocked. "Distributing child pornography."

No more than ten minutes after he had been dispatched into a police van and taken into custody, an ambulance raced into Fairhaven's car park and two paramedics were checking in at reception. I briefly wondered what that could be about, but the minute I got to my next lesson and checked my emails I saw that another pupil in my form, Kyle, had broken a teacher's foot and given her a concussion.

Apparently he thought it would be hilarious to move her chair just before she sat on it and, far be it from the wholesome prank you'd have with your teenage mates, the teacher in question fell like a sack of shit knocking herself unconscious in the process. When she came to she was in immense discomfort and couldn't walk.

I had Kyle in my lessons for the rest of the day, and sat at the back of the room keeping a lower profile than a billionaire at the end of the tax year. When I found out which teacher it was, I felt like giving him a hi-five more than anything. Miss Lewis was one of the most obnoxious people I'd ever met, enthralled with the idea that all the kids loved the sarcastic persona she'd created for herself, when in actual fact she was more of a condescending bully than an educator. She'd moved Kyle's chair as he was about to sit down earlier on in the lesson, and all he was doing was returning the favour. The fact she'd fallen like one of the twin towers and damaged herself in the process wasn't his fault, he was merely copying the behaviour she'd set out.

In the space of a single day I'd had to deal with a revenge porn victim, a boy who will now have to spend five years on a sex offenders register, and a kid in my form who'd hospitalised a member of staff. They don't warn you about any of that on the "Get Into Teaching" adverts.

For the next week or so I kept a close eye on Myley. It was nigh on impossible to imagine what she must be going through, but I knew that keeping tabs on her was the right thing to do. Schools can often feel like political war zones, where alliances are made, friends become enemies and enemies become friends on a near daily basis. Now with the popularity of social media, the bullying and the name calling doesn't end at 3pm. I spoke to her Head of Year and a couple of her teachers too for good measure, we were a network of eyes tracking her movements and making sure this wasn't too much for her to handle.

We needn't have worried. Within just a couple of days the old Myley was back, as noisy and as hyperactive as ever. Rather than live in shame, she'd embraced the exposure and was now going through what appeared to be a phase of sexual liberation. She had more interest from boys, many of which found her confidence especially alluring, and she'd become a fountain of knowledge for the girls, who were bombarding her with questions they'd been pondering throughout their pubescence.

You couldn't help but sit back and admire Myley. She had a remarkable way of taking bad experiences, grabbing them with both hands, wringing them dry of all positive outcomes like a damp cloth, before discarding them from her life. She took an experience that would crush most people and manipulated it entirely to her own advantage. You can't help but feel somewhat in awe of a teenager with more resilience than most adults.

For several days she was the talk of the staff room as we all hypothesised what we would do had we been in her situation at that age. "Well I've never even sent a dick pick", said Mr Kitson confidently, before adding "the zoom on my camera's not good enough."

CHAPTER 20

Fights were a common occurrence at Fairhaven. The kids were a little tougher, their reputation that little bit more important to protect. I guess when you're growing up and you don't have much, even something as silly as having a name for yourself as being tough is worth keeping. It wasn't just the boys either, the girls fought just as much and were often far worse. It feels as though when two males fight there's an unwritten code of honour amongst them - no punching in the dick, no attacking from behind, no weapons. But with the ladies, nothing is off limits. They will pull hair, they will use their nails, they will gouge eyes and kick shins and use their bags like a medieval knight with a ball and chain flail. Boys fight like rhinos; they size each other up, face their adversary down and charge towards one another. Girls fight like putting two angry cats in a pillowcase.

Very rarely is a fight between two bullies, it's much more common for it to be between two people from different year groups or between a bully and someone who's had enough of taking their shit. Wilson, the kid from Haiti, had found life difficult at his new school. He was an outsider, didn't really fit into any social groups, and was often on his own at break and lunch. Because of this a few of the boys in his year had started picking on him. Naturally as a teacher you try and look out for this sort of thing and put a stop to it but the sad fact of the matter is you can't watch them every minute of every day.

One boy, Slater, had a particular penchant for picking on Wilson. He was a cocky child from a rough family in one of the shittiest council estates in the area. A lot of students feared Slater, who in turn propagated this reign of terror by being a nasty little fucker to almost everyone he met. On a particularly wet afternoon in February, Slater pushed Wilson's buttons a little too hard and Wilson, according to an eye-witness pupil at the scene, "absolutely twatted him".

Gossip travels like wildfire in schools and before long everyone knew the story. Slater had stolen Wilson's bag and proceeded to throw the contents all over the floor. Wilson rugby tackled him to the ground, pinned him down and punched him in the face a few times, breaking Slater's nose.

While Slater lay on the ground wondering what the hell just happened, Wilson decided to climb onto an outdoor table and, in a move taken straight from the WWE, jumped onto Slater like a human cannonball. That evening myself and a few other staff stayed late so we could watch the whole thing on CCTV. Wilson was a big boy and the impact he caused with his kamikaze dive onto Slater looked seismic.

"Jesus Christ" said one of the teachers, "first they had a hurricane, now I bet the shock waves from that jump have probably caused an earthquake in Haiti as well."

The following day Nina swung by my classroom unannounced to "check how things were going". I'd been at the school for five months, and this is the first time she'd checked up on me like this. In fact, she hadn't really offered me any kind of support whatsoever. Had it not been for Alina, I would have been fucked from day one. I was suspicious - had she been tipped off by the clique? Was there something I had done wrong and she was giving me the opportunity to confess?

"Oh by the way, I just wanted you to know that we're interviewing for your job next month and I was giving you a heads up in case you wanted to apply."

So they were going to make me interview for the job that I currently had, just like they did with the last teacher. I felt disheartened; it wasn't like I was doing a bad job or anything, the kids liked me, I'd kept up to date with all my work, I was punctual and polite, what more did they want?

When I spoke to Alina about it, she was more pragmatic in her analysis. "At the end of the year they'll have to increase your salary, so they make you re-apply for your job just in case they can get someone else in to do it cheaper. They need to save money at this school any way they can"

she explained. Of course, whilst my job was now up for grabs, Lauren had managed to keep hers. When it came down to a choice between me and her, I stood no chance. She had the clique behind her.

It took me a few days to get over the shock of my job no longer being secure. I knew it was nothing personal, it was a cost cutting measure. Hell, just a few days ago Nina had scolded a member of staff for printing out two extra "spare" worksheets for her class. If everyone did that for every lesson, she reasoned, our department would be losing hundreds of pounds a year. When budgets are stretched as tightly as this, it's little wonder I was deemed as replaceable.

Once I'd got my head around this, I decided to reapply for my job the next chance I had. But that free moment never came. Any time I set aside time to fill out the application form, something else got in the way. I ended up doing marking instead, or planning lessons, or creating worksheets and new activities, or ringing parents, or doing a litany of other jobs that a teacher is expected to squeeze into a day. For some reason, applying for my own job never made it to the top of my to-do list.

Perhaps subconsciously my brain was delaying me from coming to a conclusion that had been brewing for months at the back of my mind - that I just wasn't cut out to be a teacher. Every time I worked on my comedy, every hour I spent driving to gigs or writing material or putting dates in my diary, this was all time I could have been spending making my lessons better, getting on top with my marking, delivering the best standard of education possible to the children that needed it most. I was conflicted; on the one hand teaching afforded me so much satisfaction and personal fulfilment, but on the other it was becoming increasingly obvious I couldn't do both.

Maybe Linda had been right this whole time.

In my heart I knew I really wanted to continue teaching. For all it's downsides, it was an immensely rewarding job. I loved being in a classroom, but I hated the politics of the staff room. The paranoia that comes along with the job is incredible, usually I'd have to inhale a few joints of Amsterdam's finest to get this irrationally anxious. Everywhere I went I felt as though I was treading on eggshells. And perhaps the worst part was that I knew this wasn't something that was going to change. I wasn't willing to live a life of constantly looking over my shoulder like I'd grassed on a mob boss and was in some half-arsed witness protection scheme. I wanted to continue teaching, but I didn't want it to be in this department.

A couple of weeks went by before Nina once again swung by my classroom unannounced, popping up out of nowhere like athlete's foot, only far more irritating. "I just wanted you to know the applications close this week and we still haven't had yours." She declared. Nina often spoke in passive aggressive tones like this, and it took a while for you to tune into the subtext of her conversations.

"Thanks," I responded cautiously, "but I've given it some thought and I've decided I'm not going to put myself forward." I was purposely blunt with her. Just because Nina spoke in riddles she assumed everyone else did, often you'd speak to her candidly about a topic and she'd extrapolate all sorts of hidden meaning from it that was never your intention. Managing the clique had made her paranoid. I knew that she saw the way they'd bullied out other members of staff and, if I had to guess, I'd say she was terrified of them turning on her. Perhaps she thought that Deputy Head of Department Zoe might one day make a power grab, and because of that she was constantly on high alert.

Nina was clearly taken aback. "Well, we're still going to go ahead with the interview process" she said, like this was some bizarre double bluff on my part, as if I was some shrewd poker player who was pretending to fold to see what his adversaries would do. I explained that I understood her position, and thanked her for checking up on me. She left my classroom speechless, and no doubt a little bit in shock.

For the rest of my time at Fairhaven I was shunned by most of the department. Nina effectively ignored me, which was ideal because it kept her off my back. The clique pretended I didn't exist at all, only speaking to me out of professional necessity and not for general politeness. They'd never start a conversation with me or try to engage me with anything they were doing. I was very much an outsider looking in. It felt like being punished by the Amish community.

The only person who continued to recognise my existence was Alina, and truth be told I could see in her eyes she was hurt and upset that I was leaving. I think she'd maybe envisaged an uprising, that me and her were going to form some sort of alliance and take back the department like a staff room Star Wars. Instead I'd tapped out the first chance I got, not even fighting to retain the position I had. I couldn't shake the feeling that Alina was disappointed in me, she was just too nice of a person to say so.

Ironically, with Nina and the clique off my back my enjoyment of the job improved dramatically. I no longer had to second guess myself, nobody was breathing down my neck, I didn't have a target on my back. If I fucked up, so what? What were they going to do, kick me out a few months early and get a supply teacher in? Of course not. Because of this I taught with a freedom I hadn't felt since Moorfields, and my lessons were better as a result. It just goes to show, if you micromanage your staff within an inch of their lives and make them terrified of slipping up, you won't get the same results as if you just trust your employees and let them get on with it. I can't help feeling that's a morale not exclusive to teaching.

I still needed to formally tender my resignation to the headteacher, Mrs Mason. I waited until the very last day before the Easter holiday and, in an act of cowardice I would live to regret, I put the letter on her desk at the end of the day when I knew she wouldn't be around. Mrs Mason was a truly inspirational woman, someone who'd given her life to levelling the playing field for the children in the area.

She'd worked tirelessly for decades for the poor and disadvantaged - Lancashire's very own Mother Teresa. I couldn't bring myself to look her in the eye and tell her that I couldn't make the same sacrifices she had. That I wanted to make pissed audiences laugh more than I wanted to make deprived children learn. It felt like such a selfish, shameful thing to do.

As soon as I'd arrived home I had a phone call from Mrs Mason, who was every bit as wonderful and empathetic and understanding as you could ever hope a boss to be. She took time out of her day to tell me how impressed she'd been with my teaching, how much she felt like the pupils at the school looked up to me, and how dedicated I'd been to doing right by them. Furthermore, she wished me all the best in my comedy and said she'd loved seeing how my background had shaped my teaching style.

This got me a little teary eyed, she was the first person to embrace my stand up heritage and see it as an asset, rather than this ugly secret that needed containing at all costs.

Fairhaven was by no means a perfect school, but it had perfect leadership.

CHAPTER 21

Once you've decided to leave a school, you can't let your pupils know until the very last possible moment. When students get wind of your impending departure, it's open season to disregard anything and everything you say. In their eyes you're no longer a teacher, no more a permanent fixture of their lives and thus not worthy of deference. It's worth pointing out that not all kids feel this way; there are many exceptionally polite and considerate young adults who'd show you respect regardless of your position in the school. But the ones with more challenging behaviour, they *need* to see you as a teacher. The minute they sense your position has been compromised, that's when they become even harder to discipline. Their minds become infested with the educational equivalent of "you're not my real dad".

It takes a surprising amount of mental fortitude to keep a secret like that from all of the children, particularly the ones you've developed a bond with. You have to come to work every day and put on a mask to keep your emotions in check. It helps to remind yourself how important the stability of the school environment is for some of these kids. In a world where their parents are inconsistent, different family members keep looking after them, they have different routines and bed times, they sleep in different beds, school is the one constant. It's the anchor in a sea of change.

So when something big happens at your school that rapidly changes everything around you, the aftershocks are not just felt among the staff. All of the pupils have to live with the disruption, and some cope better than others. In early May, just after the bank holiday, Mrs Mason called all staff in for an emergency meeting. As the main hall swelled with every member of faculty plus all additional support staff, nobody had a feeling that it was going to be good news.

As Mrs Mason made her way onto the podium, there was a solemn look in her face which I hadn't yet observed. "We've had the call." She said. That was all that was needed. Nobody questioned what "the call" was or what "the call" was about. Everyone in education knows what "the call" means - OFSTED are coming to visit.

There was a shell-shocked hush that rang around the room. Within a few seconds, the hall sprung into life, a cacophony of questions and concerns erupted and the room that was silent moments ago transformed into a veritable rainforest of chirps and howls. Mrs Mason explained briefly that we were to go into our own departments and do whatever we needed to do to make sure the school retained its "Good" rating. This included, but was not limited to, making sure that every book was marked up to date and adhered perfectly to the school's marking policy, ensuring every lesson for the next two days was of an outstanding quality, with printed lesson plans for each just in case, knowing the names of every pupil we taught that had SEN (special educational needs) and making sure all wall displays were neat and tidy and classrooms and corridors were free from clutter.

This was the first time I'd experienced an OFSTED visit. What struck me immediately was the sense of camaraderie it evokes, as soon as we got back to our departments the clique were already offering their services to anyone that needed help. These were staff members who hadn't so much as asked me how I was for three months, now all of a sudden they were offering to fix my wall displays and tidy my room. At times like this, office politics are pushed to one side.

OFSTED doesn't judge the individual. Either we all pass, or we all fail.

I left the school that night at 11.30pm and was back the next morning at 7am. Whilst at home I barely slept, I kept imagining someone was going to break into my room during the night and rip down all the wall displays and Tipp-ex all the marking out of my books like a reverse version of The Elves And the Shoemaker. I thought I'd be the only one in school at this time save for some senior members of management, but almost half the teachers were already there. Nina had left school at midnight and was back in for 6am, her paranoia firmly in overdrive as she rustled through the classrooms one by one like a truffle pig sniffing out anything that might warrant her attention.

Three inspectors arrived at exactly 8.30am, each dressed sharply in greys and muted blacks, each carrying clipboards and briefcases. Pleasantries were exchanged via a formal handshake, their expert poker faces maintaining total neutrality at all times. I reckoned I could have gone over there and smack one of them straight in the genitals and he'd have barely batted an eyelid. Being near them was haunting, in a way. They looked like the Dementors from Harry Potter if they stopped guarding Azkaban and started working for the Inland Revenue.

For the rest of the day I was on tenterhooks. At any moment OFSTED inspectors could burst into the room unannounced and demand my books and lesson plans, scrutinising them for any discrepancies that could bring the overall grade of the school down. At lunchtime, two inspectors came into my room. Turns out they weren't particularly interested in judging a school by the quality of its new teachers, but were very interested in speaking to me about the support I was getting from staff.

"Can you describe what it's like working in the department?" A wiry grey man asked.

"Oh, it's brilliant, everyone is SO nice." I lied. Alina was nice. Lauren had her moments. But the clique were nasty bitches and Nina was like working for a conspiracy theorist on meth.

"Do you feel you're getting enough support from the school?" He continued.

"Absolutely," I lied again, "Nina checks up on me regularly and I know I can come to anyone if I have a problem". In reality Nina hadn't checked up on me in months and coming to anyone with a problem was the equivalent of signing a document allowing someone to come and shout at you for half an hour.

"What would you change about Fairhaven?"

I paused for a moment, choosing my words carefully. "I'd change the amount of funding the school received. They do so much here with so little, I think if there was more money available then they could do even more for their pupils." It was the classic technique of using a negative to highlight a positive, sort of like when an interviewer asks you what your greatest weaknesses are and you tell them you're a perfectionist that works too hard.

They asked a couple more questions about the school and the behaviour of the pupils and I once again lied through my bare teeth to paint the school in as positive a light as I could. I could have told them about the uglier parts of Fairhaven, the department in turmoil, the staff bullying, the re-listing of my job to save a bit of money here and there, but it never for a minute crossed my mind to undermine the school like that. It felt like I'd have been stabbing everyone in the back, and I couldn't do that to anyone, least of all Mrs Mason.

No sooner had the inspectors left my classroom, Nina practically burst through the doors demanding to know anything and everything that was said. She must have been worried because I was leaving, thinking that I might throw her under the bus. Part of me really, really wanted to fuck with her - "I told them you drink on the job Nina" - but I couldn't bring myself to do it,
Nina was a stressed out mess at the best of times, but the extra pressure of the OFSTED visit had pushed her into a meltdown so big it would give Chernobyl a run for it's money.

If there's one good thing to come from an OFSTED inspection, it's watching the school put on a show for the visitors. Everyone comes together so that they see the school on it's very best day. The inspectors aren't stupid, they know what's going on, but they can only judge according to what they see. Even the kids get in on the act - you'll see some of the most troublesome pupils acting like little darlings, answering questions and handing out books and being model citizens instead of the miniature criminals you're accustomed to. I saw a boy in Year 9 hold a door open for an inspector; the same boy whose parents I had to call a week earlier because he was grabbing tufts of his pubes and putting them on the shoulders of his female classmates.

By the time the inspection was over, I had a sneaking suspicion that we might have just gotten away with it. Our department was running more smoothly than ever, and the kids had behaved impeccably throughout. No fights, no swearing, not so much as running in the corridors. It was as close to perfect as we were ever going to get. A few days later, we got the news to say the school had retained it's "Good" status, and everyone breathed a huge sigh of relief. We could relax for another five years.

Personally, there was no doubt in my mind that Fairhaven was a good school. It might have been a little rough around the edges, the pupils were challenging, the budget was tighter than a camel's arse in a sandstorm, parts of the building were in desperate need of repair and the clique ran my department with a mafia-like precision that was so well-drilled I'm surprised Martin Scorsese isn't making a film about them. But despite all that, what they did with the pupils that came through their doors was genuinely incredible.

It reminded me of a TV show where they take old, clapped-out cars and fully restore them to their original glory. Cars that anyone else would have overlooked. Cars that most people would sell for scrap metal, because it's easier and nobody has the time needed to refurbish them. That's what the school felt like to me; we were taking kids that were on the fringes of mainstream education and giving them the opportunity to get themselves the qualifications they needed to go to college or do whatever they wanted in life. Some grabbed it with both hands, some we could never get on board. But at least they all got the chance.

I often thought about St Matthews, and how they would turn away problem children who didn't meet their religious criteria for the sake of keeping the school's grades intact. Then I would think about just how bad a pupil would have to be before Fairhaven decided they were a lost hope.

One pupil that sprang to mind was Kayla - the girl who once couldn't go more than a day without being suspended had calmed down dramatically since the turn of the year. Her grandfather had passed away over Christmas and she'd been very close with him. Before he died, he'd spoken to her about the importance of educating yourself and making the most of the time you had, and that was all she needed to hear. Slightly perplexing for me, because I'd literally screamed those words at her face dozens of times - "It's FREE education! How are you so determined not to take advantage of it?! There're children in other countries that work for pennies in a factory doing 20 hour days, they'd give their right arms to go to school!" - but I guess sometimes it's not just about hearing the right words, they need to come from the right person.

It was only in the final week of my time at Fairhaven that I told my classes I'd be leaving. Lucky Carla didn't work here, otherwise she'd have blurted it out months ago along with my comedy background, a link to all my videos, my mobile number, credit rating and home address. The reaction of the children was difficult, most were upset, a couple were fucking ecstatic, and there was more crying than I'd anticipated. One boy in a Year 8 class who was incredibly quiet and polite just burst into tears. I honestly didn't expect that from him, and I don't think he expected it from himself either. I didn't think I'd made any sort of an impact on him either, I'd always got the feeling he was pretty nonplussed in the lessons, but clearly I'd meant more to him than he let on. That's one of the more profound things about this job, you'll never truly know just how much you meant to some of the kids you taught.

I'd expected the initial reaction would be of shock, and then the kids would quickly adjust and within a few hours they would not give even the slightest of shits. But this wasn't to be the case - throughout the week pupils were making time out of their day to come and see me off, even ones that I didn't teach. Some were asking me to fulfil cheeky requests for them, and most of the time I duly obliged, like a Poundland genie in a lamp that could only grant the most basic wishes. Can you bring in some sweets for our last class? Done. Can we call you Hagrid to your face? No problem. Can we shave your beard off? Absolutely not.

One girl, Lola, asked me to sing an Ed Sheeran song for her. She'd been a huge fan of the singer since I'd started teaching her, sporting an Ed Sheeran backpack and Ed Sheeran pencil case to solidify her devotion to the pop singer. She'd even tried to dye her hair ginger in tribute until her mum got wise and told her she'd get grounded. I had to decline, given that most of Ed's hits are love songs and an overweight bearded man serenading a 13 year old girl to a love ballad isn't exactly the strongest look to go out on. Instead I bought her an Ed Sheeran pencil sharpener. It cost the grand total of 30p and yet she treasured it like it was front row tickets to see the man himself.

A Year 10 pupil named Stewart was absent on my final day but wanted to say his goodbyes personally, so another member of the class facetimed him so that he could speak to me. He didn't say an awful lot, given the effort he'd gone to just to talk to me, and he was calling from somewhere familiar that I couldn't quite make out. At the end of the call, his friend told me the reason for his absence was because he was in hospital; the previous night he'd been out late and gotten himself into an altercation with another man who'd stabbed him in the arse. He'd managed to hobble to the now ironically named walk in centre who'd stitched him back together, presumably as opposed to letting him live out the rest of his days with two arse holes. He phoned his parents to say he was staying over at a friend's house, and they assumed he was in school right now. This was his life, at fifteen years old.

The reactions among the staff was far more of a mixed bag. Most of the staff wished me well, some with more sincerity than others. A few were flat out jealous of me being able to abandon the profession and make money from comedy. "I don't fucking blame yah mate" said the unfortunately named Mr Bonce, Head of Year 8, "get out while you can. I mean that. It's a raw deal is teaching. You work your fucking arse off and every year you get told you ain't doing enough. If it's not the kids it's the parents, and if it's not the parents it's the school, and if it's not the school it's the government, and if it's not the government it's the media. I remember 30 years ago, you told someone you were a teacher they'd look at you with respect like if you were a banker. Nowadays you tell someone you're a teacher they look at you like you're some sort of prick, like a banker."

I thought about what Mr Bonce had said. Here was a man who'd clearly fallen out of love with teaching and yet, because he'd been doing it for so long, he didn't have anything else to fall back on. What else was he going to do in his late 50s? Suddenly retrain as something else and spend the next few years at the bottom of a corporate ladder? Of course not. Far better he kept his head down and taught Science for his remaining few years before slipping into retirement. Mr Bonce was trapped in teaching, the same way those old comics were trapped on the circuit. I guess that's something that can happen in any profession, but at least in comedy you don't have to deal with hundreds of teenagers calling you Mr Nonce for 35 years.

Alina bought me a bottle of wine as a parting gift. "I'm pretty sure it's against my religion to even buy this," she said, "but fuck it, I won't tell if you won't." The wine itself was a cheap Merlot, but often it's less about the gift and more about what it represents, and this represented that she was willing to risk a lifetime of eternal damnation for me, which was really rather sweet of her. Nina said her goodbyes as a formality rather than anything else, checking I'd completed all my marking and left the room in a reasonable state. It was more like being checked over by a landlord to see if you get your deposit back than it was a sincere moment of well-wishing.

The clique continued to ignore my presence, except for Lauren who came over and had a brief chat with me. She really seemed like a nice woman who'd, for want of a better word, fallen in with the wrong crowd. I told her that I hoped she had a long and successful career, and she said the same for me. It's a jarring feeling when you see the seeds of friendship just beginning to bud when you're already heading out the door.

On the final day, after all the pupils had gone, I went round my classroom one final time to check I hadn't left anything. What shocked me was the amount of stuff I'd bought for the classroom with my own money. A box of two hundred pens. £19.99. Easily worth twenty quid to not have to deal with kids pissing about looking for something to write with every lesson. Whiteboard markers. A fiver. You get a pack of four for that price and it'll last you a term. Coloured sheets of A3 paper I bought from an art shop so we could do more group activities like at Moorfields. Post-it notes. Stickers. Glue sticks. Scissors. Practically everything in here was mine. There was easily a hundred quid's worth of stock here, and that was what was left over from the end of a school year, so Christ knows how much more I'd spent to replace things that had broken or gone missing.

You don't realise at the time just how much of a teacher's own money gets spent on improving their lessons. You don't get reimbursed for it, you can't claim it back at the end of the year as a taxable expense. In fact, you don't even really think about it while you're buying it. Your brain just goes "my class needs more paper, I'll go out and buy some", never for a moment stopping to think that maybe it should be the school or the government that funds the learning materials needed to teach a class effectively, and not your own pocket. There's even a thing called "Poundland

Pedagogy", where every year teachers will go on social media and share things they've found in Pound shops and how they plan to incorporate them into their lessons.

The more I found in the classroom that belonged to me, the more it seemed unfair to take it. What was I going to do with a dozen packs of post it notes anyway? Spice up the old love life by sticking them all to my body and performing the least erotic strip tease known to man for my girlfriend? At least here they'd be used. As I went over to my desk for the final time, I saw that someone had left an envelope for me. On the front they'd written "Dear Hagrid." Opening the envelope, I saw a card inside.

Dear Sir,

I just wanted to say how sad I am that you're leaving and how happy I am that you were my teacher. English has always been my hardest subject and you helped me through it and gave me all the extra help I needed when I was stuck and I will never forget that. It hasn't been an easy year for me with everything what has happened and I know you know what I'm talking about and I wanted to say that it helped me knowing that you were there and that you didn't look at me different when a lot of other people did. It was hard to come into school for a long time after that but I kept going in because I didn't want to let you down. I hope you enjoy whatever you do next with your life because you helped me enjoy mine. One of my friends says you're a comedian but your not funny so I don't know.

Thank you again,

Myla.

My heart swelled. As teachers from time to time you can't help but sit back and you wonder whether or not you're actually making a difference in anyone's life, whether you're a role model to them or an inspiration or a calming influence, or if you even make a dent in their lives whatsoever. Whether your presence has made a permanent mark on who they are as people and who they will grow up to become, or whether you're merely a bug squashed on the windscreen of their world. This was proof, undeniable, objective proof, that I made a lasting difference to at least one person.

On the other hand, she also used the wrong "you're" in the last sentence, so I can't have been that good.

About a week after I'd finished school, I was in my local pub with a couple of friends, remarking about how much shittier a pub is during the summer holidays when the kids are off. Children of all ages were running around, screaming and shouting, pestering their parents who were trying desperately to ignore them and shoo them away. All the while we're sat here, three grown childless men in our 30s, trying to enjoy a pint and wallow in abject misery that keeps being spoiled by the ubiquitous ebullience of youth.

"Six weeks of this shit" said Andy, who worked in a factory pressing sheet metal.

"Why do they even need six weeks holiday anyway?" Asked Simon, lunging at the opportunity to partake in his favourite pastime of complaining about things he doesn't fully understand. Brexit was a golden age for him in that regard.

"It's the teachers," Andy concluded, "they come in at 9 and they leave at 3 and they expect all summer off so they can go on holiday."

Simon murmured in agreement. I kept my mouth shut, I knew that there was nothing I could say that would change the view they had that teachers work six hour days and lead this extravagant jet setting lifestyle. In reality, I worked more hours than Andy in his factory job and got paid considerably less. That's not to say I didn't begrudge Andy his salary, but if you're not going to compensate teachers financially then perhaps at the very least they should command our utmost respect. After all, I think we can agree that educating the next generation bears a greater responsibility than pressing the sheet metal used as the casing for hand dryers in toilets.

One of the many problems teaching faces is an image crisis. They no longer garner the same deference as doctors and nurses, and within the pages of the right-wing tabloid newspapers are often fetishised as lazy lefties who are more concerned with their next paycheck than the welfare of their students. This is categorically untrue - in my time in schools I've dealt with all different types of teachers; the overly keen ones, the jaded ones, the clinging-onto-retirement ones, the ones give every waking moment to the job, the ones that try and climb the ladder as fast as they can, but I have never, ever, heard of a teacher that's just in it for the money. They don't exist.

Why would they? The 'money' is fucking appalling. Starting salaries for teachers work out at less per hour than a manager at Greggs. There are no teachers that are just in it for the money in the same way that there aren't any molecular microbiologists that are just in it for the pussy.

The lack of money is a problem all in itself. Education is in somewhat of a recruitment crisis, as more and more graduates are looking at the job and seeing it as a raw deal. Crap pay, 50-60 hour weeks, tons of stress and you get less respect than Rodney Dangerfield. Which is a pity, because if you can see past all that, being a teacher is the most rewarding job you can have (just not financially). Let me tell you, I have stood on stage at the Royal Albert Hall in front of thousands of people laughing and clapping, and I have stood in front of one child who finally gets something that had previously eluded him and I can tell you with certainty that these two feelings are one and the same.

There are days when everything that possibly can go wrong, does go wrong. There are times when you'll want to throw the towel in, and nights when you drive home with the radio off because you're too mentally exhausted to listen to anything. And when you go through those patches, you'll have the support from colleagues who'll pull you through. Teaching is a team game. Yes it's frustrating, and draining, and time-consuming, but it is never boring. There's simply no time to be bored. Even your very worst days will fly by in the blink of an eye. If you want a job that is constantly pushing you and challenging you and gives you the feeling of knowing you're making a difference in the world, teaching is the job for you.

We can all remember the teachers from our youth. Those we loved, those we loathed, the funny teachers and the shouty teachers and the might-just-have-a-breakdown-if-you-push-them-hard-enough teachers. As time goes on you think about them less and less, but they never go away, they lurk in the back of your mind, shadows of memories of the way people used to be. Even after you leave the profession, and one day slip the mortal coil, your spirit remains in the minds that you helped to shape.

And when all's said and done I think that's the best thing about being a teacher. The knowledge that long after you're gone, part of you will continue to live on. You become, in your own way, a legacy.

EPILOGUE

Leaving the classroom is surprisingly easier said than done. Just a few days after I'd finished teaching, I booked a two week holiday for myself and my partner - one of those "sit on a sun lounger all day and do nothing but get a tan" types of vacation. It took me three days before I was tearing my hair out with boredom. I thought I needed to go away and decompress, to lock
myself in a metaphorical air chamber in a hotel in the south of Spain with all inclusive food and drink options. By the end of the first week I was counting the days before I could come home.

I'd spend my time finding things to do, needless things, just to keep occupied. While my partner was passed out on a sun lounger, knocking back strawberry daiquiris with her skin crisping under the sun like bacon in an air fryer, I was going through my phone deleting all the pictures and apps I didn't need. When she was getting lost in a good book, I was planning home decorations and watching a Youtube video on how to grout a bathroom. On the final day, I cleaned our hotel room top to bottom.

What I quickly realised was that teaching had changed me. And I don't just mean it changed my outlook or broadened my perceptions, it literally changed who I was as a person. There are certain characteristics teachers have to have; a strong work ethic, an ability to prioritise, military grade organisation, without them the job is impossible. I found myself craving structure and routine like never before, I had an urge to busy myself with tasks and chores to make myself feel productive. Before teaching I was somebody who could happily lie in bed all morning and watch TV all afternoon. Now I was up and about at 8am every morning even when I had nowhere to be.

Perhaps most surprisingly of all, I was getting cravings for teaching. I missed the rush of planning and delivering a great lesson, engaging a class, expanding their knowledge and skills. I was getting strange withdrawal symptoms - several times I even tried to teach my partner how to play chess, only stopping when one evening she asked "what will it take to get you to stop doing this?" Maybe there's a business opportunity to be had in setting up a rehab clinic for educators. We could all sit around in a circle and introduce ourselves - "hi, I'm Freddy and it's been six months since my last lesson. My rock bottom came when my other half walked in on me trying to teach the dog what an adverb was."

For a while I experimented with different ways to get my teaching fix. I signed up to an online tutoring website teaching English to foreign students via webcam. A cousin of mine who had taught in schools in China and Saudi Arabia had once spoken to me about the difference between teaching here and overseas, but it's only through experiencing something first hand that you can truly comprehend how chasmic the contrast is. Never once did a pupil arrive so much as a minute late, or without having done all of their homework. In fact on many occasions the pupils would ask for *extra* work, and if they didn't feel like you gave them enough, they'd find something else themselves. The whole culture is different - in Japan, night classes and overnight libraries are immensely popular. Pupils will study all day, go home, then go back out and study some more.
To them, turning up to a lesson late or without the proper equipment is the equivalent of a groom turning up to a wedding without his pants on. You're embarrassing yourself, you're harming your future, and you're probably going to get a talk from an elderly relative about how you're bringing shame upon the family.

I signed up to a supply teaching agency too. Being a supply teacher has a number of significant pros and cons. The main overwhelming advantages it has is that there's no marking, no lesson planning and no meetings. You come in at half 8, you leave at five past 3. It's the same job but without the baggage. However, there are significant downsides too. For one, you're in an unfamiliar environment with no idea where anything is.

Your days are filled by constantly searching for classrooms, toilets, staff rooms, even exits. Secondly, you have no relationships with anyone, and because of that the school can feel a very lonely and unfamiliar place. With that in mind, it's very hard to get anyone to respect you. Staff treat you like some sort of pigeon that's flown into the building, shooing you around until you fly off at the end of the day never to be seen again. Children are a nightmare to discipline too - they know you don't know their name, or how to contact their parents, or even the name of their Headteacher. They know you have no power.

Perhaps the biggest con of all when being a supply teacher is the uncertainty of the job. You register with an agency, tell them when you're free, and every morning between 7.30am and 8.00am you *might* get a call to say that you're needed somewhere. If that happens, you need to be ready to leave immediately. There's no time for a shower or a coffee or a cheeky morning wank. You need to be up, fully dressed in your teacher attire, bag packed, sandwiches made, with one foot out the door. When the call comes, you never know quite what to expect. You don't know if you're walking into a top academic private school or a squalid hell hole. You don't know what subjects you'll be teaching either. It could be Spanish, Art, Music, P.E or anything else on the curriculum. On the days where the call doesn't come, you don't earn any money. It's a precarious existence.

I continued to teach on an ad-hoc basis right up until the coronavirus pandemic. As well as being an extra source of income, I enjoyed the variety it gave me. Also it felt like a good idea to keep my skills sharp, in case I should ever need them. When COVID19 ravaged the country, it ripped through the education sector with a ferocity very few could have predicted. It simply wasn't possible for secondary schools to implement all the safety measures recommended by the government. Social distancing? No chance. We cram thirty kids into a classroom at the best of times. Bubbles? Never happening. Schools are designed in a way that allows a thousand kids to move anywhere inside five minutes, they're a myriad of interconnecting corridors that you can't just cordon off. Mask wearing? Yeah right. It's hard enough getting Year 10 girls not to wear their skirts half way up their arses never mind adequate PPE.

In the coming months that followed, there was a deluge of sicknesses and absences and I found my skills as a supply teacher very much in demand, the same of which could not be said about my skills as a comic. Schools usually have an on-site cover supervisor, a person paid by them to cover any gaps left by teachers who are unable to deliver lessons for whatever reason.

Occasionally, one or two supply teachers may also be required. During COVID19, I was working at schools where the amount of supply teachers outnumbered the permanent staff. I once had to cover a physics lesson for a Year 11 class that should have been taught by the Head Of Science, only she'd had a text at ten past eight that morning whilst in the staff room, telling her she needed to go home and self-isolate. The lesson in question, the last one before their Mock Exams, was instead taught by me - a man with such a rudimentary knowledge of the subject I thought Einstein was what you say when you order one beer in Germany.

To anyone who'd spent so much as five minutes in a school it was patently obvious that the situation was unsustainable. I did my best, trying to give something back to the profession I still felt I owed so much to. In total I worked in seven schools across the North West, as secondaries everywhere tried plugging the holes in their rapidly sinking ships. My supply agency even offered me a week long placement at St Matthews - I turned it down. Shortly afterwards they rang back, telling me St Matthews remembered me but were willing to let me come back as "they're desperate." My response was short, "they might be desperate, but I'm not."

Whether or not the schools should remain open became a topic of heated political discussion.

Sadly, there were a small but vocal minority of politicians and press that implied that the reason teachers might want to close the schools is because they're lazy individuals who want a few extra weeks off. I can only assume the same people think that when firefighters ask people not to set their homes alight they're only doing so because they can't be arsed putting the blaze out. Some factions of the media tried their best to make it appear as though teachers shirked their responsibility, that they were the conscientious objectors in the war with the virus. In reality they were on the front line, and most had never worked harder.

The main aims for this book were to show teaching as it really is. The highs, the lows, and everything in between. A completely honest, unflinching account of what life in a classroom is really like. But I also wanted to tell you about some of the pupils - particularly those from disadvantaged socio-economic backgrounds. The ones that need role models, guidance, and someone who genuinely wants the best for them. We're not talking about just a few kids here either, there's tens of thousands of them up and down the country, there's whole schools teeming with children that need to be taught by people who can motivate and inspire them.

If you've read this book and thought "I quite fancy doing that", I *urge* you, get into teaching. Because right now there's a lot of young people who could really do with your help.

Printed in Dunstable, United Kingdom